WILDERNESS SURVIVAL GUIDE FOR TEENS

How to Build a Fire, Perform First Aid, Build Shelter, Forage for Food, Find Water, Handle Extreme Weather, Manage Wildlife Encounters, and Many Other Important Skills!

Rick Bayne

ISBN: 978-1-957590-36-3

For questions, email: Support@AwesomeReads.org

Please consider writing a review!

Just visit: AwesomeReads.org/review

FREE BONUS

SCAN TO GET OUR NEXT BOOK FOR FREE!

Table of Contents

INTRODUCTION

Have you ever wondered what it would be like to be stranded the way people are on survival shows? While they're heavily monitored and have a fail-safe where they can call for help at any time, you won't have that luxury if you're ever in a similar situation.

Consider this: You're on a camping trip, and you head out looking for firewood. Unfortunately, it's recently rained and the ground isn't as solid as expected. As you reach for what looks like the perfect dry log, your foot slips. Suddenly, you're sliding down a massive hill, barely missing hazards along the way. Once you reach the bottom, you evaluate yourself for injuries. Luckily, you have none; however, the way you got to your current location is impossible to travel in the opposite direction. You're stuck, and no one knows where you are. It's time to switch gears into survival mode.

Would you know what to do if this happened to you? How would you get back to your camping party? Understanding the dangers of being alone in the wilderness and how to navigate is essential to ensuring you get back to safety. Additionally, if you're isolated for an extended period, you'll need to know how to find a safe, clean source of water to ensure you remain hydrated and healthy while trying to get back to your party.

The most common theme behind every survival story is having the willpower to endure. If you don't keep your spirits up, there's a very strong chance that the circumstances will get the best of you. Tenacity is essential to ensuring your success in making it out of your survival situation as unscathed as possible. In addition, if you're in a group, you can help keep everyone else's spirits up to ensure their success as well.

One way to maintain calm is to build confidence in your skills before they're needed. It's never too soon to learn how to survive in the great outdoors under any circumstances. You'll also need to know the right way to treat the natural world by following the principles of leaving no trace. By limiting your impact on the natural world, you can keep it beautiful and safe for everyone to enjoy.

We've designed this book to give you a basic understanding of the steps you'll need to take if you're ever isolated or even lost with a group in a survival situation. In addition, we'll explore what you need to know if you're facing a natural disaster or other emergency situation at your home. Preparedness is key, and we'll ensure that you understand how to achieve an excellent level of readiness by the end of this book.

From how to build a fire to how to react during an animal encounter, we'll cover everything you need to know about outdoor survival skills, giving you the best insights possible for any adventure you take. By the time you finish this book, you'll be armed with the essential skills needed to endure the toughest challenges nature has to offer.

CHAPTER ONE: INTRODUCTION TO OUTDOOR SURVIVAL

Outdoor survival may seem like a moot point with all the luxury we experience daily; however, emergency situations can occur even when you're not camping/hiking. For example, your car could break down and you end up stranded without cell service. Because of this, it's essential to know how to survive.

Whether you're a naturalist who's gotten lost or you've been in an accident that's left you in an unknown place, you'll need these skills to get you out of a bind. With survival skills comes the need to have the appropriate mindset and attitude. Without the right combination of attitude and skills, your chances of survival become smaller and smaller.

We'll look at the importance of learning survival skills and the attitudes supporting a survival mentality. We'll also consider the basic principles of survival and the common hazards of the great outdoors.

IMPORTANCE OF OUTDOOR SURVIVAL SKILLS

You never know when you could be in a situation that requires survival skills. While you spend most of your time in comfort and security, you could face danger and uncertainty when you least expect it. Situations such as severe snowstorms, flooding, heat waves, and injuries can mean that you need to be at the top of your game.

The ultimate goal of survival skills is staying alive. This is also what makes learning these skills essential. Spending the weekend in an unfamiliar area can quickly be disastrous when the weather worsens or if you or someone in your group gets injured. You'll need to think and act quickly to ensure everyone emerges from the situation safely.

Getting Closer to Nature

When you develop your survival skills, you'll have the tools necessary to help keep you safe while getting closer to the natural world. While exploring the woods can be a fantastic experience, being prepared for the unknown never hurts anyone. There's always a chance that something could happen no matter how careful you are, so learning a few survival skills is always beneficial.

Survival skills can make your experience a lot more fun. You'll know which plants are safe to touch and how to spot signs of different animals. This knowledge will allow you to interact more with the world than if you didn't have this information.

If you've never truly interacted with nature, having survival skills will better prepare you for the experience. You'll know how to mitigate exposure to the elements and avoid potential dangers while you're outdoors.

Like most humans, you've likely grown highly accustomed to having everything within reach and not having to put much effort into obtaining essentials such as food, water, and shelter. While it may not seem like it, all that is still available in nature if you know where to look.

KEEPING THE RIGHT ATTITUDE

Having the right mindset for survival is essential when you're in a tough spot. A defeatist attitude will get you nowhere. It takes a strong-minded individual with leadership qualities to get through a survival situation. As you develop your skills, you'll also need to reflect on your current mindset and attitude to see where you can change your perspectives.

Maintain a Positive Attitude

You've probably heard this about many different scenarios: You need to keep a positive attitude to achieve success. Those who persevere are the ones who maintain an upbeat attitude and look adversity in the face without backing down. Alternatively, the people who don't make it out of survival situations are the ones who succumb to a negative mindset and give up.

When you remain positive, you become resilient, finding ways to overcome challenges that you wouldn't see with a negative outlook. Everyone faces feelings of helplessness at one time or another. It's okay to have these feelings. Just take a minute, reflect on them, and change your mindset to something more advantageous to you.

Have a Decisive Attitude

When you're faced with a survival situation, you can't be wishy-washy. Making clear, firm choices is extremely important. While you might not always make the right choices in everyday life, you have the experience necessary to evaluate the circumstances and make a judgment call. It's no different when you're in survival mode. By practicing skills and learning more about emergency circumstances, you can strengthen your confidence and your ability to overcome problems.

Not making any decision can sometimes be worse than making the wrong decision. Although it's important to consider all aspects of your situation before acting, you should be confident enough to make a call and follow through with it.

Believe in Yourself

Having faith in yourself and your abilities is also important during survival scenarios. In many cases, we rely on others to get through tough spots. This may not be possible when facing a survival situation.

You'll need to believe in yourself. You can practice this in preparation for one of these situations by being more self-aware and evaluating things from different perspectives. Take control, and don't be afraid to fend for yourself when the going gets tough.

Stay Calm, No Matter What

People will often panic in crisis or survival situations. This is the absolute wrong solution. You need to keep a calm head about yourself, focusing on your surroundings and what you can do to get out of your current circumstances. Staying calm will allow you to see more opportunities and take control of the situation.

Be Adaptable

You can't be stuck in your ways when you're in survival mode. Learning how to change with your circumstances is essential. If something you're doing isn't working, you need to know when to let it go in favor of a different process that will serve you better.

Consider how plants and animals have adapted throughout history. Their survival depended on these adaptations. You'll thrive in any survival situation by keeping your mind open to change and altering your behavior as needed.

BASIC PRINCIPLES OF SURVIVAL

There are several survival concepts that can guide how you should react in any outdoor emergency situation. These principles identify key components that you will need to focus on in your efforts to make it through the event successfully.

S.T.O.P.

S.T.O.P. is a common acronym that stands for "Stop, Think, Observe, and Plan." The very first thing you need to do when something goes wrong is stop. Don't run around, retrace your steps, or panic. Doing any of these can result in worsening your situation. For example, if you are stranded and try to find your way back before stopping, you might end up even more lost than before.

Instead, take some time to think. Your brain is your biggest asset while you are in the wilderness. Try to identify where you are, if possible. If you can't determine your current location, begin working on a plan.

Next, observe your surroundings and consider the group you're in if you aren't traveling alone. You'll need to look for things you can use such as a place to shelter or something to make a signal. Additionally, you need to see if anyone is hurt.

Finally, continue working out the plan. Whatever the circumstances are, you need to have a plan of action to prepare for what's coming next.

Administer First Aid

If you or anyone with you is injured, a major priority is giving first aid treatment. You'll need to clean any cuts and bandage them with what you have available.

You'll also need to watch for complications caused by the environment, which can include heat exhaustion and hypothermia, depending on where you're located. Ensure everyone is staying hydrated.

Find Shelter

Once everyone's first aid needs are addressed, you must find adequate shelter. If you can find something that's already established, that's great. Otherwise, you'll have to construct your own shelter using what you have available in nature.

You'll need to protect everyone from the wind and the ground, the two biggest leeches of heat from the human body. Your shelter should also be as small as possible to conserve the maximum amount of body heat. If you have any materials with you, such as a poncho, you can use these to construct your shelter.

Start a Fire

In addition to shelter, you'll need a fire. Fire will serve multiple purposes at this stage of your survival strategy. One that is often overlooked is brightening the spirits of everyone in the situation. As mentioned earlier, you'll need the fire for warmth and, if anyone gets wet, drying out clothing.

Signal for Help

Finding someone lost in the wilderness can be challenging if they don't help rescuers identify their location. For this reason, you need to signal where you are. Use whatever methods you have at your disposal. This can even include your cell phone if it has a signal. If not, you'll need to get creative.

Any colorful clothing you have at your disposal can be spread across a clearing where it's easy to spot. You can place shiny objects where the sun will catch them. One of the most popular options is a signal fire, which has been used throughout history to notify rescuers of someone's location.

Stay Hydrated

It's critical to stay hydrated. You can only go so many days, possibly up to a week, without clean, drinkable water. Dehydration can also lead to illnesses and decreased ability to function. You need to be at the top of your game in a survival situation, so make sure you find a viable water source as soon as possible and drink up.

Don't Stress About Food

While being hungry isn't at the top of anyone's to-do list, having food isn't immediately essential for survival. You can go a couple of weeks without food before severe problems arise. This means you should focus on the previous principles of survival, ensuring you have all those bases covered before you begin to worry about food.

COMMON OUTDOOR HAZARDS

While you're in survival mode, there are many common outdoor hazards to be aware of. These can severely impact your health and safety while you're trying to navigate the wilderness.

Wildlife

Not all wildlife is cute and cuddly. Many animals such as bears pose a threat to your well-being. Even feeding smaller, less threatening animals can place them or your camp at risk by creating a dependency on humans. Knowing how to handle the approach of any dangerous wildlife is essential to any outdoor adventure, whether you're in survival mode or just on vacation.

Rivers and Streams

If you find yourself in a situation where you need to cross a river or a stream, you need to take care. Just because the water is only knee deep doesn't mean it can't sweep you off your feet. Look for the slowest-moving section of water, even if it's the broadest part of the waterway. This will ensure you have the safest path to cross.

Lightning

While all storms pose a hazard for a person in survival mode, you should be especially vigilant when there's lightning. It's better to take cover in a forest than under one single tree. Additionally, the top of a mountain, the crest of a ridge, and a meadow are all the worst places to weather storms.

Extreme Temperatures

Extreme hot and cold temperatures can be seriously dangerous for someone trying to survive in the wilderness. You'll need to protect yourself from the sun as much as possible to prevent heat exhaustion and dehydration. When the temperature drops, find shelter and make a fire to prevent hypothermia. Avoiding these two extremes will help you make it through your experience more efficiently.

CHAPTER TWO: PREPARING FOR OUTDOOR ADVENTURES

When preparing for your outdoor adventure, you'll likely be excited as you look forward to the fun you'll have in the wilderness. However, there are a few things you should take care of before you set out.

Packing for success on your adventure is crucial. You'll need all the important basics in the event that something goes wrong. While you hope for the best on every excursion, you must still plan for the unexpected. Packing survival essentials will ensure you're prepared for anything.

Depending on the season and the location you're traveling to, you'll need to pack the right clothing. You don't want to arrive dressed for the summer when it's a chilly 45 degrees. In addition, when you prepare for winter weather, you need to have the right materials to keep you warm and dry.

Before you head out, you should also take the time to learn some important navigational skills. Even if you pack the tools, they won't do you any good if you don't know how to use them.

Learn how to interpret the weather before you go. If you don't understand what the weather forecast means, it won't help you very much. Understanding the important terminology used in a weather forecast is essential to ensure you can plan accordingly for your outing.

In this chapter, we'll explore the essentials you need to pack for survival and clothing. We'll also cover the important navigational tools and techniques that can help you out when you're in a bind. Finally, we'll cover the terms you need to know to understand a weather forecast.

PACKING ESSENTIALS FOR SURVIVAL

When you plan to go on an outdoor adventure, it's critical to pack certain essentials for survival. Many call this their survival kit. It contains specific items that will keep you safe if something goes wrong during your outing. These items are the bare minimum that you should consider bringing with you.

Map and Compass

Technology is great... when it works. While you're out in the woods, your cell phone may not have service, leaving you stranded when you need it most. That's why having a map and compass with you is critical. Going one step further, knowing how to use both is even more important.

First Aid Kit

You never know when an injury will happen, and bandages aren't available in the wilderness. Keeping cuts clean is essential to preventing infection. All the essential first-aid supplies will ensure you're prepared for anything.

Water Purification Method

Having access to clean water is essential. When you have the time to prepare for going into the wilderness, you can pack your own water-purification system. This will help alleviate the need to find the cleanest water as it will remove the impurities in the water you find. As a backup, you should also consider bringing water-purification tablets if your other system fails.

Something To Start a Fire

If you learned how to start a fire from what's available in nature, that's great. However, you can pack matches or a lighter in your survival pack. When you can plan out your trip in advance, you have the advantage of preparing for anything. Starting a fire with a match or a lighter is much easier than rubbing sticks together.

A Knife

When you're stuck in the wilderness, having a sharp knife is essential for many different tasks. It can be used for preparing bandages, sharpening sticks for various reasons, and even skinning fish. It's a tool you won't want to be without.

Solar Blanket

Hypothermia is a serious risk when the sun goes down, especially if your clothes have gotten wet. Bringing a solar blanket can keep you warm when the temperatures drastically drop. They're also easy to pack and light to carry, making them the optimal choice.

CLOTHING FOR DIFFERENT WEATHER CONDITIONS

When planning an outdoor adventure, the surrounding environment will determine what kind of clothing you need to pack. Summer gear won't serve you well in a winter climate. Checking the weather forecast for the area you'll be in is essential to being the most prepared for your experience.

Warm-Weather Clothing

It's ideal to layer your clothing since weather can change. This means wearing tank tops or shorts underneath long-sleeve pants and shirts. A sweater and windbreaker or raincoat are also a good idea. Long pants/shirts will protect your skin from bugs and poisonous plants. Tank tops, T-shirts, and biking shorts will allow you to strip down if you're too hot.

You'll also want comfortable pants to wear on your hikes through the woods. Flexibility is essential to get the most movement. Consider options with fitted ankles, or tuck your socks over the ankles for the ultimate protection against ticks and other insects.

Your shoes should be durable with closed toes and heels. They should also offer excellent stability while you're traversing the wilderness. The last thing you want is a sprained ankle because your shoes let you down.

Cold-Weather Clothing

In the winter, things are a bit different. You'll want to plan on layers that also wick moisture, preventing sweating that could lead to hypothermia. To achieve this, you'll need a base layer to wick moisture, a middle layer that insulates, and a weather-resistant outer layer. Pack clothing that fits each characteristic.

Wool socks or wool with a synthetic blend are ideal for wicking moisture and keeping your feet dry during winter outdoor adventures. They'll keep your feet warm, while cotton alternatives will hold the moisture close to your skin, quickly turning the inside of your shoes into a frigid ice box.

Hats, scarves, and gloves are also essentials. Wool and synthetic blends are excellent options for hats. The materials you choose for your gloves will depend on the location and weather conditions you are heading into. Opting for waterproof material may be the ideal solution as a preventative measure if you're unsure.

When it comes to your footwear, you'll need something to keep your feet warm and give you excellent traction on the snow and ice. Make sure to choose boots that are waterproof.

NAVIGATIONAL TOOLS AND TECHNIQUES

When embarking on an outdoor adventure, you should know how to use navigational tools and techniques in case you get lost or accidentally stray off the designated path. If you're uncomfortable with one option, there are several others you can choose from.

Trail Markers, Blazes, and Signs

If you're hiking on a well-established trail, you'll periodically see trail markers or trail blazes indicating the correct way to go. They'll also tell you where your current location is. These markers are usually no more than 500 to 1,000 feet apart. If you've gone further than this without seeing one, chances are you've gone off course and need to turn around. Many trails also feature signs that tell you directions and distances to the next destination. These signs are typically located at a crossroads where you can take different routes.

Maps and Compasses

Before you head out on your adventure, it's best to get familiar with the area you'll be in by reviewing a map. Plotting out the exact location and identifying any landmarks nearby will help you if you become lost while you're there. In addition, bringing a compass will assist you with finding north so that you can identify your location in relation to what you're looking at on your map.

Reading the Stars

Using the stars to navigate is an age-old technique. The first thing you'll need to do is locate the Big Dipper and, from there, find the North Star. After you find these two iconic celestial markers, you can navigate your way through the wilderness toward your destination.

Natural Indicators

In the northern hemisphere, you can use a few natural indicators to help you gauge which way is north. First, you'll find moss is typically greener and thicker on the southern-facing side of tree trunks. Additionally, the bark is duller on the northern side of the trunk, and the branches reach upward on this side.

Smartphone

There's a slim chance that you can use your smartphone in the wilderness. There are often no towers, restricting access to the required signal to access any GPS apps. However, if you can use your device, it can help you easily navigate your way back to your intended location.

UNDERSTANDING WEATHER FORECASTS

The weather forecast can be a bit confusing with all the terminology thrown around. Once you get the hang of the essential terms, it makes a lot more sense when you listen to the report to plan your outdoor adventure.

Sky Condition

Sky condition describes the percentage of the sky covered by opaque clouds. However, this term may be omitted if there is a high probability of precipitation, such as 60 percent or greater, as that would suggest strong cloud cover.

Temperature

In a weather forecast, the temperature can be used in multiple ways. The first is a description of the maximum and minimum temperatures of the day, which are respectively known as the high and low. The weather person may provide a temperature at a specific time, such as when they are delivering the report.

Precipitation Probability

The probability of precipitation, or POP, is the likelihood a measurable amount of liquid precipitation will occur during a specified period at any given location within the forecast area. It's expressed as a percentage. It must be equal to or greater than 0.01 inches of precipitation to be measurable.

CHAPTER THREE: BUILDING A SHELTER

One of the first things you'll need to do in a survival situation is build yourself a shelter. The ideal shelter will keep you warm and protected from the elements. This includes the wind and the cold of the ground. It will also keep your body heat in, preserving your warmth in the chill of the night.

You should choose an ideal location that offers protection and safety. The best-case scenario will be a shelter that's ready to go and doesn't need to be built. It should also be in the driest location possible. Choosing high ground is great when the temperature isn't too cold.

Sometimes, when you're unexpectedly placed into a survival situation, you won't have a tent or existing form of shelter. You'll need to construct a shelter from natural materials in these situations.

For example, this could happen if you're stranded and a storm suddenly rolls in. No matter the reason, you'll need to be prepared for this type of circumstance so that you can build a sturdy emergency shelter to see you through.

We'll explore the different types of shelters you may need to construct and how to choose the best location. In addition, we'll also examine the best natural materials to use.

TYPES OF SHELTERS

When you're in a survival situation, the shelter you choose to build is only limited by your imagination. If you have materials with you that you can use, it will open up more possibilities than if you have to rely on nature alone.

Lean-To Shelter

You can build a lean-to if you have a tarp, poncho, or something similar. Alternatively, you can use debris you find throughout the woods. A lean-to is a structure that is generally open on three sides but offers some protection from the elements. However, you may find it doesn't keep you dry in wet weather since it only offers one side of protection.

A-Frame Shelter

An A-frame shelter is a step up from a lean-to because it has two sides. It can be made from a tarp or debris and offers better heat-retaining capacity. When built properly, it can keep you dry even during the wettest weather.

Cocoon Shelter

When you've got no other option as the night grows closer, you can whip up a shelter from leaves and debris. It won't have any framework but will function much like a sleeping bag. This isn't a good solution for the long term but will do in a pinch.

Fallen Tree

A fallen tree offers one of the easiest solutions to finding shelter since you won't have to expend energy to build it. You'll need a tree or tree branch that's large enough to crawl under or inside. The compact space will allow you to retain body heat better than other shelter options.

A Cave or Hollow

Sometimes, you'll come across a cave or hollowed-out section of rock where you can set up camp. It will protect you from the elements and allow you to safely build a fire beside your shelter. You'll have the ability to stay warm and safe simultaneously.

CHOOSING A LOCATION

When choosing your shelter's location, you need to consider several important factors. However, there may be situations where you need to bed down quickly such as when darkness is falling.

Once you have more time to evaluate the situation, you can find a better spot to establish your shelter.

Find a Dry Area

One of the key factors in choosing a proper location is ensuring it's dry. When you're wet, you'll lose body heat quickly. Even if it's getting dark, you can't afford to bed down in an area where the ground is wet, and you won't be able to use soggy debris to build. If you haven't found a way to start a fire yet, you won't be able to dry your clothing, which could result in you getting severely ill. Your survival skills will be diminished by illness.

In addition, if the area is wet, you'll likely have trouble starting the fire that you need for heat and cooking. Without a fire, you'll face additional complications. So, when you're scouting out your shelter location, you first want to ensure it's in a dry area.

Avoid Hazards as Much as Possible

Once you find a dry location that looks promising for a shelter, it's important to go a few steps further to evaluate it for safety. Start by looking up at the trees. Do you see any dead branches hanging? These are one of the deadliest hazards in the forest and are known for causing serious harm when they fall, including the death of those they land on. If you see dead branches overhead, moving on to a different location is best.

You'll also want to look for signs of rain runoff. If bad weather moves in while you're bedded down, it could be catastrophic if you're in the wrong location. Gullies and ditches can turn into nightmare situations with fast-moving water that can literally sweep you away. While a log and a long line of rocks may look like a great shelter, consider if your design will be an equally great funnel for water.

In addition, you don't want to place yourself at the bottom of a hill. Rock falls, avalanches, and landslides can occur anytime. Check the base of a hill for signs of loose debris that could indicate the potential for any of these catastrophes to happen.

These potential hazards make climbing to higher ground a beneficial tactic. Colder air will settle to the bottom of the hill at night, making the top of the hill a warmer spot. However, the higher you climb, the more exposure to wind you'll have. In addition, the ground tends to be uneven at the top of a hill, making it harder to build a shelter. The best option is to choose a spot in the center of the hill that compensates for warmer temperatures and reduced wind.

Choose the Ideal Orientation

You'll need to ensure the entrance to your shelter is pointed in the right direction. If you need to wake up first thing in the morning, you can easily direct it toward the rising sun. Most importantly, keep a barrier between you and the wind to prevent the chill from reaching you.

Additionally, where you place your fire in reference to the opening is crucial. You don't want smoke and embers blowing constantly into your face as you try to sleep. At the same time, you don't want your heat source too far away from your shelter. Choose a spot that allows the heat to enter the structure while maintaining proper ventilation.

Stay Close to Drinkable Water

Water and shelter are both critical to your survival, so keeping your shelter within very close distance to your drinkable water source just makes sense. You'll have easy access to your water when you need it without having to walk miles to locate it again.

However, at the same time, you don't want to be too close that you could be in danger. For example, you don't want to sleep right next to the water because a storm can cause it to rise or have increased wave activity. Either situation will result in you getting wet or your shelter being destroyed.

CONSTRUCTING A SHELTER WITH NATURAL MATERIALS

If you're not lucky enough to have materials with you to construct a shelter, you'll need to forage and find good natural materials that can be used for that purpose. You can use plenty of objects to build a shelter with natural materials.

It's important to note that preparing for a survival situation will benefit you greatly if you're stranded without shelter. Having tools like a knife available will make things much easier when preparing your materials.

The lean-to is the most basic type of shelter and one of the easiest to build. When you find the correct location and frame the structure appropriately, it can successfully shield you from the wind and rain. In addition, if you build it with a fire on one side, the combination can be enough to keep you insulated and alive throughout your ordeal.

1. Fix a Ridge Pole

In this first step, you'll need to find two sturdy trees that are spaced approximately one body length apart. This spacing will allow you to have enough room in your constructed shelter to stretch out fully. The best trees for this are those with forked branches that can easily support your ridge pole.

Once the supporting trees are identified, it's time to pick out the ridge pole. The branch that will serve this purpose must be relatively strong because it will bear almost all your shelter's weight. Choose your piece of wood so that it is roughly three inches in diameter, which is about the thickness of your wrist.

Next, place each end of the ridge pole between the trees' forked branches. Ensure it is jammed in securely. An alternative is using lash the pole to the tree trunks.

For lashing, paracord and strong twine are both excellent options if you have them. If not, consider tearing strips of cloth or fabric to create cordage. Bushcrafters are known for creating natural cordage from various items, including grasses, nettles, and inner tree bark.

2. Design the Lean-To Structure

You'll need several staves that will be placed against the ridge pole. They must be spaced equally down its length. These staves must have enough length to extend at a slant from the ridge pole to the ground. Once this is done, you'll have the skeletal part of your lean-to. The staves don't have to be nearly as strong as the branch you selected for your ridge pole.

Dig the ends of the staves into the ground, forming a neat row. Take a minute to verify that you will fit beneath the structure and be protected from the elements. Now's the time to make any necessary adjustments before construction progresses too far.

3. Lash Horizontal Spars

In this step, you will need to identify flexible branches to create horizontal spars to cross your vertical staves. These spars will weave above and below each stave and may need to be lashed to the end staves.

The best lashing technique to use is square or Japanese. If you are unfamiliar with either of these lashings, you can use the knots you are most comfortable with. The goal is simply to ensure a solid connection.

4. Fill in the Lean-To Frame

Next, you'll need to find many thinner branches that you can weave between the staves to fill in the lean-to frame. In the best-case scenario, they'll be as long as the spars. However, if you need to use shorter branches, that's fine as well. You'll be placing them anywhere you see gaps. The ultimate goal of this step is to create a closely knit structure that can support a roof made of leaves and debris.

5. Lock Off the Ridge Pole

Now that the basic frame is complete, you'll need another branch to secure the ridge pole to the supporting trees. This branch will prevent high winds from causing the shelter to move or collapse. Choose a long, sturdy branch, then jam it securely between the forks of the two trees your ridge pole is being held by. You will need to ensure it is lengthwise beside the ridge pole and lying over the top of the vertical staves. This is the best way to make a solidly locked-together structure.

6. Build a Roof

Starting from the ground, work your way to the top of the lean-to structure, adding layers of large bracken ferns along the structure's length. The bracken should have the stems pointed upward and the fronds downward, allowing the rain to easily run off your structure. The stems can be woven into the frame, ensuring the bracken remains in place. When bracken is unavailable, search for leafy twigs and branches to use before piling leaf litter and debris on top.

7. Add Side Walls

While most lean-to structures don't have side walls, you can easily add some to your shelter. This addition will follow a similar method to the construction of the roof. You'll create a frame, but it will be between the shelter's roof and the tree trunks this time.

Then you'll weave in the bracken as before. You can create one or two walls, depending on your needs and the direction of the wind.

8. Create a Sleeping Platform

Clear all twigs, stones, and debris from the area within your shelter to create a level, flat area. Next, fill in the space with leaves, bracken, or similar debris. Ensure you layer it thickly for maximum comfort and insulation from the ground.

BUILDING A SHELTER UNDER TIME PRESSURE

When you're in survival mode, you need to think quickly and plan where you'll post up for the duration of your situation. Creating an emergency shelter is essential for successfully making it through your ordeal.

The lean-to that we just described is one of the most commonly created emergency shelters that survivalists rely on because of how easy it is to construct. Another is the A-frame, which you can easily build without rope or cordage. When night or a storm is quickly moving in, this is a great option to get you out of the weather. Follow these steps to quickly build an A-frame shelter:

1. Choose a sturdy branch as your ridge pole. You're looking for something that's at least twice your height. Prop one end between a heavy rock and the other between the intersection of two Y-shaped branches that measure three feet tall. You can also set the base of the ridge pole in the fork of a tree if you can find one.
2. Lean branches against both sides of your ridge pole, covering its entire length.
3. Pile debris across the top of the A-frame. Your goal should be a minimum of three to four feet deep.

4. Make a sleeping pallet inside the shelter using the same material you piled on top of the frame. You'll need this to be a minimum of two feet deep to ensure you are insulated from the ground.

This type of shelter will be low to the ground, helping you keep your body heat inside. There will only be enough room for you to fit inside. You will not have significant room to move around, but the point is to have a spot out of the elements where you can stay warm and dry.

CHAPTER FOUR: WATER COLLECTION AND PURIFICATION

When you're in survival mode, one of the first things you need to do is find a source of drinkable water. While this is much easier said than done, many water sources exist in the wilderness. By knowing where and how to look for water, you'll have a much better chance of finding it right away, no matter where you are.

However, not all water is safe to drink as you find it. Even though you may be limited in your tools, there are natural ways to filter water. Regardless of where it comes from, it's a lot safer for you if you filter it.

The last thing you need while on your own in the wilderness is to get a waterborne illness. These can lead to catastrophic consequences for your health and well-being under the best circumstances. Avoiding these illnesses is essential to ensure you get through your situation.

In this chapter, we'll explore how to find water and how you can purify or filter it. We'll also examine the different waterborne illnesses and how to prevent them.

FINDING WATER SOURCES

If you suddenly find yourself alone in the wilderness with no supplies, finding water sources is one of the first things you need to do. You can only go a few days without adequate hydration. Understanding where you're likely to find water and knowing whether it will be safe to drink are essential survival skills.

Lakes, Rivers, Streams, and Ponds

The best and safest option for a natural water source that you can drink from is flowing water. More specifically, you'll want to look for small streams first and rivers second. Streams are less likely to have pollutants than larger rivers.

If either option is unavailable, the second-best selection is a lake or pond. However, because they are stagnant, these options pose a higher risk of having bacterial impurities.

Finding any of these water sources can be as easy as closing your eyes and listening to your surroundings. You'll hear the water running in a river or stream if you're lucky. Otherwise, you'll have to do some more work.

Animal tracks have a high potential of leading you to water; however, take care that you don't get even more lost when following these tracks. In places where insect swarms are particularly thick, there's an increased potential for water to be nearby. As a last-ditch effort, track your way downward. Water flows in a downward direction, so getting to the bottom of a gully or valley can help you find water more easily.

Fruits and Vegetables

Many different fruits and vegetables are an excellent source of water. These include pulpy plants, cacti, and roots. To harvest the water, you'll need to collect the items in a container and smash them. While it won't result in a significant amount of water, in a survival situation, every bit counts.

Tree Crotches and Rock Crevices

Like fruits and vegetation, you won't get a lot of water from tree crotches or rock crevices; however, when you're stranded, you'll be glad you found it. In a very dry area, seeing bird droppings around a rock crevice is a great indication there may be water inside even if you can't see it.

To collect water from these small spaces, stick the cleanest piece of clothing you have into the crevice, soak up the moisture, and wring it out into a container to collect the water. You should be able to return to this location following a rainstorm to collect more water.

Snow and Ice

If you're out in the wilderness during the winter, you may have access to snow and ice. While your first thought may be that you can just eat it, that's not the best solution. You'll need to find a way to melt it. If you have any other water available, it's best to mix a little of it with the ice or snow before melting it over heat.

Directly consuming snow or ice can lead to decreased body temperature. Because of this, it's advisable to melt it and heat it slightly to ensure your body doesn't experience any kind of shock. When your body temperature lowers, your metabolic rate will increase to help stabilize your temperature. This process results in further dehydration.

Digging Wells

In a desert-specific location, dampness or green vegetation on the ground is a sign you should dig in that spot. Dig out a large hole that's a few feet deep and the result will likely be water seeping in. Other spots to try include the bases of cliffs, dry riverbeds, and low areas or valleys. If you are successful, the water will be very muddy and require purification.

When you're stranded near saltwater, you're not out of luck when it comes to drinking water. At approximately 100 feet from the shore and behind the first sand dune, dig a hole that measures three to five feet deep. Line the bottom with rocks and the walls with wood. Your most likely source of wood will be driftwood.

With the rocks and wood in place, your hole can fill with water without the risk of collapsing or getting too much sand in your water. Within a few hours, the well will be full of fresh water. It will be a combination of rainwater and ocean water that's been filtered by the sand. If the water is salty, you must move further away from the shore to prevent ingesting too much salt.

Don't Turn to Water Substitutes

Many claim there are effective water substitutes that you can survive on when absolutely necessary. There are several reasons why these substitutes aren't healthy and should be avoided. They include the following:

- Urine has 2 percent salt content and contains bodily waste that can be significantly harmful to your health.
- Blood can transmit diseases and has a high salt content.
- Seawater has 4 percent salt content, so it requires more water to flush this out of your body than it can provide for you in return.

DIFFERENT WAYS TO COLLECT AND TREAT WATER

When you find your water source, you'll need to have a method of collecting and treating it. Ensuring your water is drinkable is essential.

Boiling Water

One of the easiest ways to remove impurities from your water is by boiling it; however, this requires you to have a fireproof container to hold the water over the fire. You'll need to boil the water for at least 20 minutes to thoroughly purify it.

You can also use this method with an alternative container if you can construct something that will hold water with natural materials. You can use material such as pine bark, but in this case, you won't be able to directly boil the container.

You may even get lucky and find something that's been thrown away such as an old bowl. Unfortunately, not everyone is considerate of the natural world, and a lot of trash is available. However, this can help you in your survival situation.

If you have a water source, the container can be used to collect water from it. Alternatively, you can set your container out to capture rainwater. With either option, you'll need to purify the water before drinking it to ensure the safest results.

Follow these steps to boil water with a container that can't be placed directly into the fire:

1. Create a container.
2. Start a contained, controlled fire.
3. Heat rocks in the fire.
4. Put the heated rocks in the container with the water to start the boiling process.
5. Continue adding rocks to keep the water boiling.

Survival Straws

Survival straws are something you'll need to have with you in your pack. They make an excellent addition to any survival kit. The straw contains a filter that can be used to drink directly from water sources. Most of these filters are equipped with advanced filters that remove harmful bacteria.

SODIS (Solar Water Disinfection)

Using the sun's energy to disinfect water is called solar water disinfection, or SODIS. The most commonly used method is exposing plastic bottles of potentially contaminated water to the sun's UV rays for at least one day. UV light will kill or damage nearly all the water's biological impurities.

This method is highly advantageous since it's easy to use and offers a good form of bacterial and viral disinfection. There's no need to use dangerous chemicals, and once you put the water in the sun, there's nothing else for you to do but wait.

The downside to this method is the requirement for sunny weather. It will also work with overcast skies, but you will need at least two days to reach maximum effectiveness. The process will not work in the rain, and no residual disinfection exists. The water and bottle must both be clear, and the bottle should be plastic. In addition, it's dependent on you finding or already having a usable plastic bottle.

Disinfecting Tablets

If you have access to disinfecting tablets in your survival kit, many of them are more than 99 percent effective at purifying water and removing pathogens. You'll want to research which ones are the best option before you stock up on these effective tools. Some work in less than 40 minutes, while others take as long as 4 hours. You'll also want to ensure you don't buy more than you'll need according to the shelf life. Using a tablet is as simple as placing it in a container of water and waiting the required period before consuming it.

WATERBORNE ILLNESSES AND PREVENTION

Waterborne illnesses can be deadly. The purpose of seeking out water is to prevent dehydration; however, waterborne illnesses can also cause it. Four of the most common waterborne illnesses include the following:

- Cryptosporidiosis
- Cyclosporiasis
- Norovirus
- Shigellosis

All four of these illnesses have the same deadly symptom—diarrhea. When you're in a survival situation and you have diarrhea, you could face severe dehydration. Some of these illnesses cause such intense symptoms that patients often need hospitalization; however, you won't have that option in survival mode.

To prevent these illnesses, there are several things you can do. First, inspect the area around any body of water before you drink. For rivers and streams, the further upstream you go, the less likely you are to encounter contamination. You'll want to look for signs of dead animals. If you were led to the water by animal tracks, move away from the area where they meet the water. Animals are may defecate and urinate where they drink, making the water potentially unsafe for you.

The next thing you'll want to do is ensure you're filtering your water the best that you can given your circumstances. Whether you boil it or use the SODIS method, taking steps to remove any impurities is essential to preventing waterborne illnesses.

MAKING A SOLAR STILL

Solar stills can help you collect water from the harshest conditions imaginable. A still works when solar energy heats the ground as it passes through a clear plastic barrier. The soil's moisture evaporates and condenses before being collected on the underside of the plastic barrier overhead.

You'll need the following items to make a solar still:

- A sheet of plastic that measures 6 feet by 6 feet
- A collection container
- Rocks

- Loose vegetation
- Optional: plastic tube, shovel, and tape

Follow these steps to construct your solar still:

1. Dig a pit that's roughly 4 feet by 3 feet.
2. Dig a small hole in the center of the pit and place the container inside it.
3. If you're using the optional plastic tube, place one end in the container and run the other end to the outside of the pit. You can use the tape to hold it in place.
4. Place the loose vegetation inside the pit around, but not blocking, the container.
5. Cover the pit with the plastic sheet, keeping it from touching the bottom. Use rocks to anchor the corners of the sheet.
6. Place one small rock directly over the container on top of the plastic sheet. Press down gently until the plastic slopes at a 45-degree angle.
7. Secure the sheet thoroughly with rocks and dirt.
8. Close the end of the tubing with a knot.
9. Wait 24 to 48 hours for the process to work. Don't remove the plastic at any time as that will result in moisture loss.

A solar still will evaporate impure water, leaving only the cleaner water behind. Impurities will be removed, making the water safer to drink. However, as you can see from the materials required, some preparation is involved. You'll need to have certain items already available to create this device.

CHAPTER FIVE: BUILDING AND MAINTAINING A FIRE

A fire is an important tool to have during your survival situation. It will keep you warm, dry your clothes, and signal to rescue workers where you're located. When it's cold, you'll need warmth, especially if you don't have any extra clothes to layer.

Knowing how to safely build a fire is critical. The last thing you want to do is start a wildfire when all you're trying to do is get warm. You'll need to have a strong understanding of fire safety and regulations before you head out into the wilderness.

Containing your fire to a pit is a great method of keeping things under control. You'll need to know what kind of firewood is the best and how to collect it. Knowing different fire-starting techniques is also essential to ensure you'll have the best chances of survival.

In this chapter, we'll explore fire safety and how to build a fire pit. Then we'll look at the different fire-starting methods you can use to stay warm during your survival situation.

FIRE SAFETY

You'll need to keep up with fire safety and regulations when using a fire. It's important to know the right way to do things to ensure your health and the safety of the wilderness around you.

Use Containment

Before starting your fire, you'll have to decide how to contain it. Popular options are fire rings and pits. The safer of the two is a pit because it's controlled below ground level, making it less likely to spread in windy conditions.

There should be a 10-foot area around the pit that's free and clear of anything that could catch fire. If you place your shelter near the fire within this area, ensure it's far enough away that it won't catch fire and that the wind is not blowing the flames toward it.

Always Put the Fire Out Before You Leave

Whenever you're leaving your shelter site, it's crucial to thoroughly put your fire out. You must never leave a fire unattended because anything could happen quickly. To properly extinguish a fire, dump water on it, stir the water into the ashes, and then dump more water on it. There should be no heat remaining in the area when you're done. If there is, you cannot leave. A small breeze could reignite your fire and cause it to spread.

Be Mindful of Your Lighting Device

No matter what method you use to light your fire, it's critical that you are mindful of the tool used. If you happen to have matches available, don't just throw the spent match on the ground. The best option would be to throw it into the fire. Otherwise, you'll need to ensure it's completely out and not a fire risk. For any other option, use the utmost precaution to prevent the spread of your fire.

Build a Safe Fire

You don't need a roaring fire to stay warm, no matter how cold it is. Start small and use dried leaves to start the fire. Add kindling and small sticks to the fire to begin building it up. Then, to add a longer burning time, add thicker logs slowly to the flames.

When picking out the spot for your fire, you must inspect the area. There shouldn't be excessive deadwood around that could cause a fire to spread quickly. You also want to avoid areas with low-lying branches that could easily catch fire.

BUILDING A FIRE PIT

As mentioned, using a fire pit is the safest way to have a fire in a survival situation. It's the least likely way to have a fire spread.

Construction of the Fire Pit

Once you have identified the perfect location for your fire pit that follows all the above safety considerations, dig out a bowl-shaped indentation that's about five inches deep. The diameter of the bowl should be about 12 inches across. This small indentation will help contain your coals while keeping them out of the wind. You'll have a bright fire with less smoke.

Using rocks, form a two-foot-diameter ring around the indentation. There should be no gaps between the rocks. Alternatively, you can use large logs to make the ring. Make sure they aren't so dry that they immediately ignite when near the fire. Additionally, avoid using rocks that have been immersed in water as heating them could cause them to explode.

Gather small brush for tinder, dry branches for kindling, and dry logs for fuel. Using the tinder and kindling, make a teepee structure. Light the center of the teepee. Once the fire is burning, add the larger logs. For a fire to last two hours, you'll need approximately five logs.

GATHERING FIREWOOD

You'll have many great options to choose from when selecting firewood in most wooded areas. When you're gathering, your main focus is ensuring the wood you pick up is dry. If it feels damp, it won't burn when you put it on your fire. In addition, it will likely put your fire out completely, leaving you to start the process over.

You'll need to spend some time foraging for the perfect wood to start and maintain a fire for the night. The last thing you'll want to do is have to get up in the middle of the night to find more firewood because you didn't collect enough before you started the fire.

While building a fire using only small twigs and fallen branches is possible, if you want it to last longer, you'll need more fuel. When looking for wood to burn, pine, ash, and birch are the best to keep a fire going. However, you'll need to keep the pieces smaller since these types of wood burn hot and fast. Smaller pieces are easier to maintain and will burn more evenly.

For longer-burning fires, maple and oak are better choices. However, you may find they're harder to light even with kindling. You'll need a well-established fire before you add either of these woods to the flames.

It's important to note that freshly cut wood can be problematic, and your go-to wood should be already dried-out deadwood. Wood that comes straight from the tree is full of moisture, and when you try to ignite it, you'll have to contend with all that water. Additionally, once the fire is finally lit, green wood tends to smoke a lot as the water essentially cooks off. It may also pop and spit, leading to the potential for secondary fires, which can be a very dangerous complication, especially if you're asleep.

DIFFERENT FIRE-STARTING METHODS

In an ideal situation, you'd have matches or a lighter with you to be able to start a fire. However, this won't be the case in most survival situations, so you'll need to know how to start a fire without any tools from home.

The Hand Drill Method

The most primitive method for starting a fire is using twigs or sticks. It's also the hardest, so if you can master this fire-starting method, you'll be an expert. Using your grit and determination, follow these steps to start your fire:

1. Start by creating a tinder nest. You'll need items that will effectively burst into flames. Consider using dry leaves, bark, or grass.
2. Next, you'll need a fireboard. Once you have it selected, cut an angular notch in it, then create a depression near the notch.
3. Place bark below the cut you made, which will be used to capture an ember from the friction generated between the stick and the fireboard.
4. Using a shaft of wood that is approximately two feet long, place it into the groove on the fireboard. Keeping the weight on the fireboard, start rolling the shaft in your hands down the axle. You'll need to continue this motion until you see an ember light on the fireboard.
5. Once you see that ember, tap the fireboard so that the ember moves to the bark. Then take the lit bark to the tinder nest. Gently blow on it to generate a fire.

The Fire Plow Method

If you haven't mastered the hand drill method, the fire plow method also uses minimal tools. You'll need softwood for the plow board and hardwood for the plow. Follow these steps to create a fire using the fire plow method:

1. Create a fireplace with a tinder nest. Select your plow board, cutting a groove in it that measures approximately one inch wide and six inches long. Then locate a piece of hardwood that is approximately one foot long and carve the end into a point.

2. Place the head of the plow on the fireboard. Rub the plow tip back and forth within the groove, creating small dust pits.
3. Place the top of the board on your knee so that it's slightly raised. This will cause the dust to collect at the bottom.
4. Once you have a small pile of dust collected, increase the momentum and force you are using on the plow until the dust begins to smolder.
5. After the dust is lit, move it to your tinder nest and gently blow on it to start your fire.

The Bow Drill Method

If you need a less demanding method for rate and weight requirements to create the needed friction for a fire, the bow drill method is the best contact-based technique to learn. The only downside is the number of materials it requires. These materials include the following:

- Fireboard: a piece of softwood that measures roughly one foot long and six inches wide
- Socket: a hand-sized flat rock with a depression on one side.
- Drill: a hardwood stick that measures approximately one foot long and one to two inches in diameter
- Bow: a green stick that is sturdy and flexible, measuring about two feet in length and one inch in diameter
- Cord: paracord or, if none is available, laces from hiking books

After you've collected all the required materials, you're ready to start your fire. Follow these steps:

1. Design the bow, which should be roughly the length of your arm. Bend it into a half-moon, tying it into position with the cord.
2. Make a tinder nest in your fireplace location. Set up your fireboard by cutting a shallow depression on its center edge.

On the board's bottom, you'll need to create a V-shaped cut that connects with the depression located on top.

3. Next, you'll string the drill by circling the bowstring around it. With the drill placed on the fireboard, use the socket to apply pressure on the other side.
4. Using the bow, begin moving the drill with a sawing motion. You should see rapid pivoting. Continue this motion until you create an ember.
5. Move the ember to the tinder nest, blowing on it gently to generate fire.

The Flint and Steel Method

For the stone and steel method, you'll need supplies from home. Many use it as a traditional fire-starting method in an ordinary campground setting. If you choose to learn this method, it's a great idea to keep steel and flint with you on any outdoor trip you take. These are the steps you'll need to follow:

1. Create a tinder nest to catch the spark you'll create with your flint and steel.
2. Hold your steel in one hand and your striker in the other.
3. Position the steel against the base to prevent movement, then push the striker smoothly down the steel's length.
4. Once an ember is created, place it in the tinder nest and blow on it gently to start a fire.

The Lens Method

To use the lens method, you'll need a lens such as a magnifying glass or binocular lens to center the sunlight on a particular spot. You'll need a significant amount of patience with this method. Follow these three steps:

1. Prepare your tinder nest.
2. Hold the lens between the sun and the tinder, looking for a bright dot to appear. Tilting the lens, ensure the dot is

directly over the tinder and approximately one-quarter inch in diameter.

3. Focus the dot in that spot for 30 to 60 seconds. Once the tinder begins smoking, gently blow on it to generate fire.

CHAPTER SIX: GATHERING AND PREPARING FOOD

When you're in a survival situation, you'll need to learn how to gather and prepare food. While this won't be your first priority, it will eventually be necessary. Understanding what's safe to eat and what's deadly is a survival skill you should develop before you embark on your outdoor adventure.

Even though it may not sound like a desirable task, you'll also need to learn how to trap and snare small game. Once you've captured an animal, you'll need to know how to prepare it. Fishing is also an ideal source of nutrition when you're out in the wilderness.

While you may know how to cook at home, cooking over an open fire is different. You'll need to master this technique to successfully prepare your food during your survival experience.

We'll explore how to identify edible plants and berries and ways to tell whether what you found is dangerous. We'll also look at the best ways to trap, snare, and fish to provide yourself with valuable nutrients. Finally, we'll discuss the best techniques for cooking over an open fire.

EDIBLE PLANTS AND BERRIES

Foraging will likely be your main source of food in a survival situation. It requires the least amount of energy and tools. However, it also carries a significant amount of risk given the number of poisonous plants and berries that grow in the wild.

Identifying Edible Berries

Berries that grow in tightly packed clusters like raspberries are considered 99 percent edible worldwide and should be your first choice when foraging for berries. Blue, black, and purple berries are also considered largely edible at 90 percent, but you're better off conducting an edibility test. Orange and red berries are risky at only 50 percent edible. Green, white, and yellow berries should be avoided since they're only 10 percent edible.

Some of the most common edible berries you may come across in the wilderness include the following:

- Raspberries
- Blackberries
- Blueberries
- Elderberries
- Wild strawberries
- Mulberries

Having a firm knowledge of what these berries look like will make it much easier to gather safe food to eat.

Identifying Edible Plants

You can also find many wild plants that are safe to eat. While it may not be the first thing you think of, there are many edible weeds in the wilderness. These include dandelions, cattails, clover, and wild mustard. You may even come across wild onions, but they can be challenging to identify.

Learn the Common Toxic Plants

Learning how to distinguish between edible and toxic plants and berries can be challenging, but there are some common toxic plants you should familiarize yourself with before heading out on your adventure. These include the following:

- Holly berries
- Poison hemlock
- Poison ivy
- Poison oak
- Poison sumac

Traits of Toxic Plants

Many dangerous plants have common characteristics that make them easily identifiable as inedible. You'll want to pay attention to any of these signs.

1. If a plant has milky sap, you will likely experience skin irritation or another kind of strong allergic reaction. This type of plant should be avoided at all costs.
2. Fine hairs and spines are a defense mechanism in most cases. Generally, they will cause a stinging or burning sensation when handled with bare skin.
3. Umbrella-shaped flower clusters indicate the plant has high toxicity.
4. When plants have wax on their leaves, it can often indicate toxicity.
5. While many mushrooms can be edible, you'll need to be careful when you find them. You should never eat a mushroom that you cannot identify with perfect certainty due to the potential for toxicity.

Methods to Identify Edible Plants and Berries

When you find food in the wild, you can conduct an edibility test to ensure it's truly safe to consume. Follow these steps:

1. Eliminate all potential food sources that meet any of the criteria for traits of toxic plants.
2. Perform a skin test by taking a piece of the plant, rubbing it on your outer lip or forearm, and waiting 15 minutes to see if you have a reaction.
3. If you don't experience a reaction to the skin test, follow it up with a taste test. Taste the exact same part of the plant and wait 15 additional minutes.
4. Next, you'll need to do a bigger taste test if there wasn't a reaction, soapy taste, or bitterness. This time, chew a teaspoon-sized amount of the same part of the plant for five

minutes, spitting out saliva as needed. Swallow after the five minutes have passed and wait for eight hours.

5. If you haven't experienced any reactions after eight hours, you can eat approximately one tablespoonful of the same part of the plant and wait another eight hours. If you don't have any reactions following that, you can consider that part of the plant edible.
6. Remember that not all plant parts are edible just because one is. You'll need to perform the edibility test for all the parts you intend to eat to confirm they're safe.

TRAPPING AND SNARING SMALL GAME

Most of the time, in a survival situation, you'll likely find yourself foraging for or eating insects. However, knowing how to set traps and snares is essential as you could find yourself capable of catching something that offers more sustenance. These are some of the easiest traps and snares you can create in the wilderness.

Simple Snare

This snare is perfect for those situations when you find an animal's den. You'll need to tie a small loop, passing the end of a wire or string through it to create a loop noose. When using string, you'll need to use sticks to keep the noose from closing on itself.

As the animal exits its den, it will get its head stuck in the noose, tightening it around its neck as it struggles. Wire works best for this situation because it stays open more easily. Additionally, it's harder for an animal to free itself from the wire.

Twitch-Up Snare

A twitch-up snare is a better option because it takes care of the additional task of killing the animal when it twitches up. This is a more humane option. Additionally, this snare throws the animal into the air, making it less likely for a predator to reach it. You will need to do some work to make this snare.

To start, you'll need to find a young sapling located on an animal's trail. Once you find that, you'll need to locate two sticks to create a trigger bar, which you will place into the ground. Next, at the top of the sapling, tie a noose and bend it down so you can lash it together with the trigger bar. The noose should be open and located over the animal's trail.

The trigger bar should be strong enough to restrain the sapling and small enough to release when an animal passes through the noose. When an animal passes through the noose, the sapling will release, sending it into the air and breaking its neck.

Deadfall Trap

A deadfall trap is fairly versatile and can be made in many different ways. No matter how you construct it, the function follows roughly the same basic idea.

You'll need a heavy object that you can prop up with an arrangement of sticks. This trap is designed so that an animal touching the sticks will cause the constructed arrangement to fall. You'll need to put bait under the trap to attract an animal. When the heavy object falls, it will crush the animal, providing you with small game.

Squirrel Pole

While squirrels are generally fast creatures that are impossible to catch, a squirrel pole will make it much easier. You'll need a diagonal branch leaned against a tree with significant squirrel activity. There will need to be many wire nooses along the length of the branch, approximately two inches in diameter and one inch away from the branch.

While traveling up or down the branch, a squirrel must travel through at least one of the nooses, causing it to become stuck. You must not place any nooses near the top or bottom of the branch. The goal is to keep the squirrel from being able to touch its feet to the ground or branch. Instead, it will strangle in the noose.

FISHING TECHNIQUES

Fishing is a great food source if you're near a clean water source. You'll need to know how to fish with the tools at hand in the wilderness. Luckily, there's generally trash laying around that can be used. While in most situations, this would be frustrating and disappointing, you can make the most of it in a survival situation.

Bottle Fish Trap

If you find a plastic bottle, you can easily construct a bottle fish trap. You'll need to cut the top off the bottle and then flip it around inside the other half. Place the transformed bottle into the water with the opening facing the current. Fish will be able to enter but not exit the bottle.

Hand Fishing

It might be surprising to know you can catch fish by hand. It's most effective in bodies of water that are full of catfish. These fish enjoy dark places. You can look for signs of them from the shore, and if you identify any holes with multiple entrances, you can quickly and quietly block one of them.

You'll need to slowly reach inside with your dominant hand, moving your fingers in a way that worms would move. The fish will bite you, so you must grab its mouth. Holding tightly, pull it from the shallow water. Catfish are known for having sharp barbells that could scratch you, so you'll need to release your grip as soon as you can get it to a safe area on shore.

Spearfishing

To spearfish, you'll need a strong piece of wood to start with. Then you'll need to add a sharp piece of metal or rock on one of the ends. Once the spear is constructed, stand over a clear body of water without casting a shadow. When a fish swims by, plunge the spear at it. This is a very challenging technique to master, but if you're in a survival situation, it's worth trying to obtain hearty fish.

Gorge Hooks

You can also use gorge hooks, which can be made from nearly anything. When you're in the wilderness, you'll need to find hard pieces of plastic, sturdy twigs, or bones and attach them to a fishing line or something similar.

The hook must be sharpened on both ends with a notch in the middle to be secured to the fishing line. If you can, attach a piece of bait to the hook. Gently lower the hook into the water and wait for a fish. When a fish comes by, you'll need to slowly pull the line, turning the gorge hook sideways to lodge in the fish's throat.

Fish Striking

Last but not least, you can resort to striking fish with a large object such as a rock or a branch in desperate times. This technique is best used in areas where you can see larger fish swimming in shallow water. You'll need to have patience and spend a lot of time practicing.

COOKING OVER AN OPEN FIRE

When you have an open fire, you can cook directly on it or around it. To cook around it, you'll need several flat stones that are preheated next to, but not within, the flames.

Once you select your rocks, thoroughly clean them to use as your cooking surface. Place the cleaned rocks right next to the fire to allow them to heat up. Once they are fully heated, place the food you want to cook directly on the rocks. This will work for any plants or meat you've collected.

Use sticks if you'd rather cook over an open flame. You'll need a long enough stick to be able to sit safely back from the fire while placing the food you are cooking over the flames. It's the same principle as roasting marshmallows, but meat or fish will be even more difficult to cook to a safe temperature.

CHAPTER SEVEN: FIRST AID

Having an injury in a survival situation can be deadly. You'll need to be prepared with first aid skills to assess and treat injuries. While you likely won't have bandages and antiseptic creams available, there are still steps you can take to ensure an injured person doesn't get an infection.

Knowing what common outdoor injuries are can help you avoid them or respond when they do occur. Before you depart for an outdoor adventure, you should create a first aid kit to take with you. Knowing the kinds of danger you could face will help you develop the best kit possible.

While being in a survival situation itself is an emergency, there are plenty of other emergencies you could face while in the wilderness. You'll need to be prepared to handle whatever comes your way.

In the following chapter, we'll discuss how to properly assess and treat injuries and what kinds of injuries are most common in outdoor situations. We'll also cover how to build the most effective first aid kit for all your outdoor adventures. Finally, we'll discuss the best ways to handle emergencies so that everyone stays calm.

ASSESSING AND TREATING INJURIES

When you're out in the wilderness, there's a strong chance that someone could be injured, and you may need to assess and treat those injuries without a first aid kit. Knowing some basic techniques before you head out is essential.

Making a Poultice

You can make a poultice for anyone suffering from inflammation or an open wound. A poultice is a paste that you apply directly to an injury to relieve the inflammation, keep it clean, and help it heal faster. Many things can cause you to need a poultice, including sharp rocks or a fall.

Several plants located in the wilderness can be used to make a homemade poultice. Once you devise the poultice, place it between a bandage and the wound. It will soothe and provide antibacterial benefits. To treat wounds, look for chickweed, red rose, and plantain. Red rose will also help stop bleeding.

Making a Splint

If you or a member of your party experiences a break or fracture, you'll need to provide basic treatment until help arrives. You can position the broken limb in a safer position, but avoid too much movement.

To minimize jostling, create a simple splint. You'll need two pieces of wood placed on either side of the injured limb. Wrap the wood pieces with paracord to complete the splint. Don't try to reset the bone yourself unless you're a trained professional. Simply immobilize it and wait for help to arrive.

Making "Stitches" or a Tourniquet

You'll need stitches if you sustain a cut that's significant enough that a bandage with pressure will not stop the bleeding. In the wilderness, it's unlikely that you'll have a suture kit and the knowledge to stitch a wound. For smaller cuts, you can use super glue as an alternative. It will need to be applied carefully and may burn; however, it will stop the bleeding.

For more severe cuts, you can fashion a tourniquet. To make one, tie a shirt or something similar just above the cut. Ensure it's tied very tightly to stop the blood flow. If you have tape, you can tape the wound shut. Tourniquets should only be used in the event of potentially life-threatening blood loss.

COMMON OUTDOOR INJURIES

Many injuries are common outdoors and can make survival very challenging. You'll need to take care to ensure that none of these happen to you or, at the very least, you have a plan for how to handle them when they do.

Sprained Ankles

A sprained ankle is perhaps the most common of all outdoor injuries. With the terrain being uneven and your mind focused elsewhere, it's easy to see why this injury happens so frequently.

If you or a member of your party sprains an ankle, the injured person will need to rest and, if possible, ice the injury. If it's winter, you can use snow or ice from your surrounding environment. Otherwise, soaking a shirt in cool water will also work. Then you'll need to apply a compress and elevate the ankle above the heart. Do this for 20 minutes, let the ankle warm up for 15 minutes, and repeat. The injured party will need to rest at least every two hours.

Cuts and Abrasions

Just like at home, when it comes to cuts and abrasions, you'll need to stop the bleeding, clean the wound, and bandage it. However, things are a bit different in the wilderness because you may not have access to everything you do at home.

For example, avoid using water you find in streams, ponds, and similar bodies of water because bacteria in the water can infect the wound. This is why it's essential to have a first aid kit with you.

The ideal cleaning solution is hydrogen peroxide or rubbing alcohol. Once it's cleaned, apply antiseptic cream and a bandage.

Head Injuries

No matter where you are, head injuries are nothing to play with. You'll need to ensure the injured person is alert. Look for severe symptoms, which can be hard to identify with a head injury.

Burns

Because you're starting your own fire, there's a chance of getting burned. Be extra careful when handling embers to generate your fire and when putting out the flames. If you do get a burn, it's important to chill it as quickly as possible. Cool water is a great option for doing this. When the wound is dry, clean and dress it.

BUILDING A FIRST AID KIT

To be the most prepared in the wilderness, you'll need a first aid kit. Creating your own is better than relying on one that's already prepared at the store.

Selecting the Bag

When choosing the ideal bag for your first aid kit, you need to consider a few important characteristics. First, most of the items in your bag must be dry and protected from the elements, so your bag should be waterproof. The last thing you need is to be caught in a severe rainstorm without shelter or fall into a body of water and have all your bandages ruined.

Second, it shouldn't be easy to puncture the bag. That would defeat the purpose of it being waterproof. Finally, it should be compact and easy to organize. You don't want to be toting around a large bag where it's hard to find anything if you need it quickly.

Trauma Items

Severe injuries can threaten a person's life, well-being, or mobility. Burns, knife wounds, or broken bones may all require professional treatment as soon as possible.

The most important items to include in your first aid kit include the following:

- Sterile heavy gauze
- Trauma pads
- Roller bandages

- Butterfly closures
- Suture kit
- Tourniquet
- Blood-clotting agent
- Burn salve

Wound Care

For less threatening wounds, the following items are the most important to consider packing:

- Nitrile gloves (multiple pairs, as you'll need new ones for every wound you clean)
- Cotton swabs
- Antiseptic wipes
- Syringe with an irrigation tip
- Tweezers
- Small scissors
- Safety pins
- Magnifying glass
- Antibiotic ointment
- Bandages
- Non-adhesive sterile wound dressings
- Medical tape
- Moleskin
- Skin glue

Breaks, Fractures, Sprains, and Strains

Preparing for potential broken bones or sprains is essential, especially if you plan to navigate rough terrain. Plan on packing the following items:

- A bendable foam-coated splint
- Triangle bandages
- Ace bandages

Medications

Having some over-the-counter medications on hand can be beneficial as well. Consider adding these items to your first aid kit:

- Antihistamines
- Pain relievers
- An EpiPen
- Anti-itch cream
- Anti-diarrheal medicine
- Antifungal cream

Additionally, if anyone in the party has their own medications, they'll need to be included.

HANDLING EMERGENCIES

Whenever an emergency arises, the number one thing to do is stay calm. You can't think if you're panicking. Even if someone is injured and it looks severe, you need to keep your wits about you and think clearly.

Stop and take time to observe the situation. Calm yourself and create a plan of action. You don't want to do anything that will make the situation worse. In many cases, when someone is injured, you'll try to stabilize them until help arrives, not create a cure for the situation.

If you don't have a first aid kit, think back to your training and use your knowledge to develop a treatment plan from the natural world around you. The most important thing is to treat the injured person quickly, stopping the blood flow and cleaning the wound to prevent an infection.

CHAPTER EIGHT: NAVIGATION AND SIGNALING

Knowing how to navigate is an essential skill to have. Getting from point A to point B without a hitch takes skill when you're in the wilderness. With many methods to find your way, you can choose the one that works best for you.

Using a map and compass is the traditional way to navigate through any terrain. However, if you become lost in the woods, you may not have this luxury. Luckily, there are many other options, from following the stars to seeing how moss grows on trees.

You'll also need to know how to signal your location so that help can find you. It's essential to do this wherever you make camp. However, you'll also need to ensure that your signal is clearly visible. Having an emergency communication device with you would be extremely beneficial, making your calls for help go through a lot more quickly and efficiently than smoke signals.

We'll cover how to use a map and compass to navigate and discuss navigating when you don't have a compass. We'll also explore how to signal for help and use emergency communication devices.

USING A MAP AND COMPASS

If you're out in the middle of nowhere and your cell phone doesn't work, you need a way to navigate. If you're lucky, you'll have a map and compass. Even better, you'll know how to use both of them well.

Basics of a Compass

When you're using a compass, there are a few basics you'll need to know to confirm you're moving in the right direction. One of the primary features is the arrow for magnetic north. This is what spins around on the dial. Generally, the tip of this arrow will be red.

There will also be a fixed arrow outside the compass compartment. This arrow shows your direction of travel and points in the same direction as the physical front of the compass. The stationary index line also points toward the front of the compass, but unlike the travel line, it is located in the spinning compartment.

The bezel ring rotates around the arrow that seeks magnetic north. It's numbered with all 360 degrees. The orienting arrow is directed at the 360-degree mark on the rotating bezel ring.

You can choose to purchase a compass with a clear baseplate so that it's easier to hold it over your map and see through it. In addition, many come with attached rulers that can be used with the map's scale to calculate distances more easily.

Understanding Magnetic Declination

Yes, your compass will always point to the north. Again, this is magnetic north, not the north on your map. You'll find there is a slight angle of difference between magnetic and true north. This angle is referred to as declination.

To put some perspective on this, some areas of Washington state have a declination of 20 degrees to the east, while some areas of Maine have a declination of 20 degrees to the west. Even one degree of miscalculation can put your entire journey off by 100 miles or more, so it's essential that you make the appropriate adjustments for declination at your location.

Central Wisconsin is the agonic line's location, known as the area of zero declination. All declination is at or very close to zero anywhere near this line. For any locations to the east or west of this line, you'll need to compensate by adding or subtracting the correct number of degrees to obtain the correct bearing. Many maps will provide the declination of an area; however, this value can update annually with the changing location of magnetic north.

How to Align the Compass

Remember that the red magnetic needle indicates which way magnetic north lies from your position. The orienting arrow is located on the housing and outlined in red. It rotates when the housing is turned. The goal of aligning the compass with magnetic north is to turn the housing until the rotating magnetic needle is seated inside this orienting arrow. Once you do this, your compass will be set to magnetic north.

How to Take a Bearing

When someone says to get their bearing from a compass, they're referring to the direction they want to go from their current location. You'll need to use the direction of travel arrow located at the front end of the compass's plate. If the index line and direction of travel arrow are connected, they are the same line.

With your compass roughly held at the mid-chest level and parallel to the ground, point this direction of travel arrow toward a landmark. Next, turn the housing until the red orienting arrow completely encompasses the red magnetic north needle. Now, determine the degree number that's paired with your direction of travel line. This is your bearing.

How To Orient Your Map

Before you can even think about reading a map, you first have to orient it. It won't do you any good if you're trying to read it upside down or sideways. To orient it, follow these steps:

1. Keeping your direction of travel arrow pointing toward the top of the map, place your compass on the map.
2. Rotate the bezel until north and the direction of travel arrow are in line.
3. Slide the baseplate all the way left or right until one of its edges meets an edge of your map, keeping the direction of travel arrow pointed toward the top.
4. Keeping the map and compass steady, turn until the needle marking magnetic north and the red orienting arrow are nested.

With your map oriented, reading it will be much easier. Landmarks should be easier to identify. You'll want to keep reading the map as you progress to make sure that you aren't straying farther from the path.

Basics of a Map

To use your map properly, you'll need to understand its basic components. These key parts include the following:

- Scale: The scale reveals how much of the area the map will show and how much detail will be revealed within that area. It's represented by a ratio. When you're on foot, you'll want a large-scale map that provides as much detail as possible. So, when preparing for your outing, consider this before you purchase your map.
- Legend: Any map worth its salt will have a legend explaining what the different symbols and measurements mean. It should contain information such as declination, map scale, and symbol charts.
- Latitude and longitude: These are the lines that run parallel to the equator (latitude) and parallel to the Greenwich line (longitude). They are used on maps to provide exact coordinates for locations.

NAVIGATING WITHOUT A COMPASS

If you don't have a compass or something happened to yours, don't worry. You'll have plenty of other options for navigation. However, you'll want to practice these before you head out camping or exploring so that you have real-world experience using them before you need to navigate in an emergency.

Using the Sun to Navigate

The sun is relatively reliable in gauging your navigational direction. We all know it rises in the east and sets in the west. In addition, when it's at its zenith in the northern hemisphere, it's actually due south. Using these basic guidelines, you can assess where you are, whether it's to the north, south, east, or west.

Using Your Wristwatch and the Sun

You'll need an analog wristwatch with hands to perform this navigational technique. When located in the northern hemisphere, direct the hour hand at the sun while maintaining the watch in a flat position. You'll need to make a line between the hour hand and 12:00. This will be your north-south line, with north leading away from the sun. At 12:00, you'll see you cannot make a line between the hands. Instead, you'll need to use the mark for 12:00 as your line.

In the southern hemisphere, point the 12:00 mark toward the sun while holding your watch flat. Make a line between the 12:00 mark and the hour hand. This line will be the north-south line, with the north leading away from the sun.

The Stick and Shadow Method

In the northern hemisphere, you'll need a long, straight, thin stick to place vertically in flat ground. Identify the end of the shadow it casts and place a marker on it. You can use something like a rock. This marker will indicate the west. Next, wait 20 to 30 minutes, placing a marker at the edge of the newly created shadow. This marker will indicate the east.

Once you have the two markers established, draw a line between them, making your east-west line. You can now bisect this line to identify the north-south line. The only problem with this method is the amount of time it takes. In addition, you could still find yourself walking in aimless circles, which means you'll have to periodically stop and make a new stick and shadow compass to correct your direction.

Using the Stars at Night

People have used the stars at night to help navigate for centuries. They are an excellent way to help orient you to the cardinal directions.

When you're in the northern hemisphere, look for the north star, whose actual name is Polaris. This star will provide you with a bearing on the direction of north. To identify the North Star, begin with finding the Big Dipper. Once you find the Big Dipper, follow an imaginary line from its two outermost stars upward until you eventually come to the North Star.

In the southern hemisphere, the popular set of stars to navigate by is the Southern Cross. This cross-like configuration is easily identifiable. Once you find it, imagine a line traveling from the top of the cross to the bottom. Continue the line south by five times the cross's height. This base of this imaginary line is a ballpark reference for the direction of south.

Using Water Features

Following water is also another recommended tactic for navigating in a survival situation. This is especially true if you are up a mountain as all streams lead downhill. You'll eventually come to a larger body of water or civilization. In addition, the waterways can be used as directional guides until you get ready to divert off the path in your next direction.

SIGNALING FOR HELP

One of the most important things you'll need to do while in a survival situation is signal for help to let your rescuers know where you are. If planes are flying overhead, you'll need a highly visible signal that can be seen from the air. In addition, if people are searching on foot, making noise can help them find you.

Use a Mirror

While it may seem silly, you should pack a signal mirror in your emergency supply kit before you head out on your trip. It's one of the farthest-reaching signals aside from electronic devices. Your small mirror has the potential to generate a beam that can be seen 10 miles away.

You must ensure you're pointing the beam of light at a target, whether it's a road or an aircraft. Hold one hand out with your fingers in a *V* shape. Holding the mirror toward the sun, reflect a beam of light across your upraised fingers.

Flash the beam to signal your distress. Angle the mirror up and down slightly to achieve this effect. If you flash three times, your signal will most likely be taken as a call for help.

Blow a Whistle

In general, yelling and screaming will get you nowhere but tired in a survival situation. While you may think you're being extremely loud and your voice is carrying, it's not going very far. Another essential item you should have in your emergency kit is a whistle. As with the mirror, three blasts of your whistle will indicate to anyone nearby that you're in distress.

Create a Message for Aircraft

If you are located anywhere near a clearing or a beach, you should establish a message for any aircraft flying overhead. It can be made out of stones, any reflective material you have, or anything fluorescent. *X* is the symbol used to indicate you need medical assistance, while *V* indicates you need help.

Make this message as big as possible. Ideally, it will be 30 to 50 feet long and have a width of 3 to 4 feet. Remember that what seems large to you on the ground will look small to those in the sky.

Use a Fire to Signal for Help

The goal of a signal fire is to produce more smoke than flame. To do this, you'll need to start a fire like normal. Then, once it's burning, add green vegetation to the flames. When planning your fire, ensure you're in an open space where it will be seen. Burning a signal fire in the depths of the woods will not be very effective since the canopy of the trees will conceal the smoke.

If you have flares with you, use them as a signal. Take care not to start a fire or injure yourself. If the area you are in is experiencing a dry season, you'll need to be extra careful about setting up your fire or using flares. One brisk wind could spread sparks, creating an uncontrollable wildfire.

EMERGENCY COMMUNICATION DEVICES

When you're in the backcountry, there's a strong possibility your cell phone or GPS devices won't work. The signal is likely to be poor due to a lack of cell towers in open land. You can consider emergency communication devices to have as a backup instead.

Two-Way Radios

With two-way radios, you can communicate with other party members, but you won't be likely to reach anyone much farther out. Some devices can reach up to 25 miles; however, the terrain and other factors can affect the signal, reducing it considerably.

When you purchase radios, ensure you get at least a pair to take advantage of all the benefits. While these units are often capable of communicating across brands, buying two of the same model will ensure they're compatible.

One-Way Satellite Messengers

Satellite devices have a much farther range when it comes to sending messages, so if you want to be able to send a message back to someone at home, consider investing in a one-way satellite messenger. Unlike a two-way radio, it doesn't suffer from the same physical limitations.

However, the downside to this option is that you can't receive a response to your message. In addition, you'll have to pay for a monthly membership to use the service.

Two-Way Satellite Messengers

An upgrade on the concept of the one-way messenger, the two-way messenger will allow you to send *and* receive messages. You'll also be able to share your location. So, if you were to become lost and someone at home had one of these messengers, you could easily relay your location, and help would be on the way.

CHAPTER NINE: SURVIVAL PSYCHOLOGY AND MENTAL HEALTH

It's easy to slip into a downward spiral when you're in a survival situation. We've all had stressful experiences where it all seemed too much to stay positive. However, the key to coping with the stress of what's happening is maintaining that positive attitude and kicking anxiety to the curb.

As hard as it may be, you can't let your circumstances get the best of you while you're trying to make it in the wilderness. The people with amazing survival stories are those who never gave up. They looked adversity in the eye and didn't back down.

It may just be you against the wilderness for a few days, but you've prepared for this. Of course, being in the situation and practicing are two different things, but all you need to do is remember what you've learned.

This chapter will explore how to cope with the stress a survival situation can cause and how to develop the mental toughness and resilience needed to overcome it. We'll also review tips to maintain a positive attitude and stay motivated throughout these difficult situations.

COPING WITH STRESS AND ANXIETY

When you're in a survival situation, the uncertainty can lead to excessive stress and anxiety. You'll have to be able to cope with both of these mental health concerns to be the most successful in your endeavors.

Identify the Signs and Symptoms

If you recognize the signs and symptoms of stress and anxiety, you can immediately begin working on handling them before they grow into something unmanageable. These indicators can include emotional responses, such as irritability, feeling overwhelmed, lack of motivation, and depression. You may also have physical reactions, including headaches, muscle tension, and a rapid heartbeat.

You'll need to establish strategies for handling stress and anxiety as soon as you notice any of these signs and symptoms. The sooner you start working on easing them out of your mind, the better off you will be.

Understand the Causes

While the entire situation may cause stress and anxiety, several other related issues can cause a spike in their activity. These issues can include mental exhaustion, physical fatigue, fear of the unknown, and a lack of resources.

Develop Resilience to Stress and Anxiety

One of the most important attributes you'll need to overcome stress and anxiety is resilience or mental toughness. It's crucial to maintaining your positive attitude and coming out on the other side of your survival situation as a winner.

Discuss the Situation

If you're not alone, it's essential that you have open communication with other members of your party. This will help keep everyone on the same page and updated with the current state of affairs.

Additionally, other people can be sounding boards when you need to vent or discuss things that are seriously bothering you. Letting things out can help reduce your stress and anxiety levels.

Take Time to Breathe

Taking breaks is okay when you're lost in the wilderness. You'll burn out if you don't leave yourself some time to think. In addition, a break is a great time to practice mindful breathing. Deep breathing has long been a trusted remedy for relieving stress. It can help recenter your mind and refocus your thoughts on what you need to do, helping you find the best solution to your problem.

Rid Yourself of Self-Defeating Thoughts

While you can be your biggest fan, at the same time, you can also be your biggest enemy. When circumstances are dire, that nagging negative voice may rear its ugly head and begin whispering in your ear. If you devise a plan for something, it may shoot you down, telling you it will never work.

Take this voice with a grain of salt, ignoring every negative thing it has to say. You can also counter it with a positive thought about how your plan will be successful because you've practiced and prepared for this day.

Despite wanting to stay within your comfort zone, the time has come to branch out far and wide. There's no time for negative thoughts; they'll only keep you from accepting challenges as they present themselves.

Acknowledge How You Feel

Your emotions are valid and shouldn't be ignored even if they're negative ones. However, don't get hooked on those negative thoughts and wallow in them. You need to acknowledge your feelings and move on from those thoughts.

Practice Self-Compassion

You're in a tough situation when survival mode kicks in. There's a lot you'll need to do to survive until someone comes to rescue you.

However, that doesn't mean you shouldn't take time out for self-compassion.

This should not be confused with self-pity. Self-compassion is when you talk to yourself, extending love and understanding. Treat yourself like you would someone you deeply care about.

Avoid Seeing Your Circumstances as Insurmountable

While being in a survival situation can seem dire sometimes, you should never look at it like it's the end of the world. That mindset will only take you down a dark road. Instead, consider it a time of change in which you must accommodate and adapt to what's happening around you.

Start by accepting that your situation is less than desirable but not insurmountable. From there, you can begin deciding your next steps, building your resilience as you continue to adapt to the challenges you're facing.

Remember that you may not be able to change the circumstances around you, but you can control how you respond to them. Keeping a positive, adaptable attitude is more likely to give you the motivation to keep pushing forward.

Stay Flexible

To develop resilience, you also need a high level of flexibility. If you can adapt easily to the circumstances you're in, you'll become more and more resilient as time passes. In a survival situation, nothing is written in stone. You may need to modify techniques you practiced in training or develop new ones as events unfold.

Staying stuck in your ways will severely limit how well you succeed. You'll need a creative mindset that allows you to develop new techniques and think outside the box. This adaptability is what gets survivors through their ordeals.

Evaluate the Challenge

Another key aspect of developing mental toughness is knowing exactly what you're up against. Not every survival situation is the same. For example, some people can become lost on a snow-covered mountain, while others go astray in the woods during the summer heat.

You'll need to take a few minutes and truly evaluate what you're facing. Plan what you'll do first before you take another step. After you've identified the extent of the challenge and what you plan to do about it, you can begin working with your new mindset.

It's also a great time to minimize the event's power over your mind. While a survival situation is overwhelming, scary, and uncertain, if you let it completely take over your mind, you won't be able to function. Take some time to establish with yourself that you're in charge.

Have Self-Confidence

It's important to maintain confidence in your mental strength. When you believe in yourself, you'll have more power over your situation. You'll even achieve more than if you didn't. Believing in yourself is the key to mental fortitude and resilience.

This will also help you branch out of your comfort zone more easily. You'll be more inclined to try things you never did before, including techniques that could help you survive.

KEEPING A POSITIVE ATTITUDE

Your positive attitude can be a game-changer. People who make it out of dire situations often talk about how hope kept them going even when they were struggling to survive.

Compartmentalize

One significant factor that can negatively affect your attitude is being overwhelmed by a complex task. For example, building a shelter involves many steps. If it's too much to handle thinking about the project as a whole, you can compartmentalize it into smaller steps. Take it one step at a time.

This can help prevent stress and anxiety, allowing you to remain positive. By focusing on one step, such as gathering materials, you don't have to think about everything that comes after. You can complete the first task, and once that's done, move onto the next step.

Express Gratitude

While this one may be a bit of a challenge, you'll want to practice gratitude as much as possible. It may not seem like you have much to be thankful for as you're scrounging around for firewood and materials to make a shelter, but there's always something.

Gratitude can increase your mental resilience. In addition, a positive mindset combined with gratitude will make stressors and challenges easier to handle. So, every time you have a win, no matter how small, recognize it. Consider things like your first fire, finishing your shelter, and finding water all things to be grateful for.

Remember That the Situation is Temporary

As hard as it may be, you'll need to remind yourself that the situation is temporary. You don't have to live the rest of your life in the woods. Consider it a test of your mettle. Once the test is over, you can go home. However, you need to visualize it to remind yourself that you won't be stuck forever.

STAYING MOTIVATED IN DIFFICULT SITUATIONS

Individual motivation in difficult situations can come from many different sources. Survivors from around the world have reported various factors that kept them going throughout their ordeals. While finding water, building shelter, and making a fire are all great goals to achieve, once you complete them, you'll need something else to hold onto.

Many have placed a lot on their personal beliefs, holding onto them dearly while on their own in the wilderness. By focusing on these beliefs, they were able to find the strength they needed to move forward with their goals for survival. Others have discussed how thinking about returning to their loved ones was enough to keep them going.

No matter what you find when you look deep inside yourself, you'll need a source of motivation. This will allow you to maintain a positive attitude and develop mental toughness.

CHAPTER TEN: WILDLIFE SAFETY AND ANIMAL ENCOUNTERS

While you're in the wilderness, there's a strong chance you'll have an animal encounter, especially as you begin searching for food. You'll need to be prepared to handle these situations in the safest way possible, whether that's avoiding animals or reacting to an encounter.

It's important to stay as safe as possible because you may not have a first aid kit available. In addition, some of these animals may cause worse injuries than a first aid kit could manage. Knowing which animals are safe and which should be avoided is essential.

In this chapter, we'll explore how to identify dangerous animals and avoid animal encounters. We'll also discuss what to do when faced with an aggressive animal. Finally, we'll delve into the basics of animal behavior.

IDENTIFYING DANGEROUS ANIMALS

Many dangerous animals exist worldwide. Knowing what they look like from a distance could help keep you safe while you're in survival mode. If you see any of these animals, you should not try to engage them, no matter how hungry you are. You will not have the tools necessary to bring them down, and the results will be catastrophic.

Bears

No matter what specific type of bear you may come across, you should consider them all dangerous. While some generally leave humans alone, they're all known for attacking given the right circumstances. You'll need to make a lot of noise when you're out foraging for supplies as a scared bear will attack.

The best decision you could make upon seeing a bear is slowly back away and avoid the situation altogether. Never run or turn your back on a bear since this may cause it to chase and attack you. In addition, you should never make eye contact because this is considered aggressive behavior.

The average bear will likely be satisfied with smelling that you're human and move onto other things. If you're faced with a grizzly, watch for signs of it charging, which will be indicated by it flattening its ears. At this point, you should lie on the ground in a submission pose while playing dead. The bear will paw at you and hopefully leave. If it doesn't, you must be prepared to fight.

Cougars

Big cats may not be seen before they attack. They find viable prey and stalk them until they feel the time is right. However, they generally don't attack humans that travel in groups of two or more.

If you are threatened by a cougar, your actions should very similar to dealing with a bear. Stand tall, keeping your eyes on the animal and never turning your back. Attempt to make yourself appear larger than the cat.

If the cougar attacks, it's essential that you don't let it take you down. You must maintain your footing. At this point, fight with everything you have to get away.

Wolves and Coyotes

Wolves and coyotes travel in packs, which makes them even more dangerous than if they were loners. They'll strategically hunt within their packs, surrounding their prey and moving in for the kill.

The ideal situation is to not get surrounded by either type of pack. If you're in an area with wolves or coyotes, be especially careful and listen for sounds of them moving closer to your area so that you can avoid them entirely.

Rattlesnakes

Luckily, a rattlesnake often announces its presence with its characteristic tail rattle. They have a natural camouflage, which makes it hard to distinguish them among the leaves and brush. It's also important to note that while an adult rattlesnake will make noise to warn off predators, it generally will not rattle before striking. However, the babies will. Rattlesnakes are venomous at any age.

Rattlesnakes love fallen logs and piles of leaves, which are two things you'll be searching for to build your fire and shelter. Because of this, you'll need to take extra care if you're in an area where rattlesnakes live.

If you see or hear one, position yourself at least six feet away to prevent yourself from being in the striking zone. Whatever you do, do not attempt to strike it with rocks or sticks to kill it or scare it away. All you'll succeed in doing is aggravating it. Instead, move away from the area to avoid the animal.

Moose, Elk, and Deer

Not every dangerous animal is a predator. Sometimes, the animals we hunt turn into violent creatures. Moose can be extremely dangerous, going so far as to kill those hunting them. These animals will kick with their front feet and then stomp on their prey with all four feet. Those with antlers will use them as deadly weapons.

Deer and elk are more likely to attack when you get too close to their babies. When deer and elk attack, it's generally from behind. Because of this, you should never turn your back on either animal. Instead, while facing the animal, spread your jacket wide to give the illusion that you're much larger than you are.

AVOIDING ANIMAL ENCOUNTERS

If you come across a wild animal, especially if it's one known to be aggressive, the best solution is to avoid the situation entirely. Because you're likely to not have much to defend yourself with, getting away before the animal notices you is the main priority.

Never Take Wildlife by Surprise

One of the biggest things to avoid is surprising wildlife. Many animals, especially bears, won't react to you unless you scare them. Once they're startled, they go into a defensive mode in which they'll attack to protect themselves even if there's no real threat.

Because of this, you should make as much noise as possible when exploring. Of course, this may be counterproductive to the hunting of game, but it will keep you safe from an animal encounter that could prove deadly.

You're more likely to alert the animals to your presence when you make noise. Because they'll realize there's a human nearby, they'll move further into the woods, more often than not, to avoid being seen. This will be the best outcome for both of you.

Avoid Getting Too Close

No matter the circumstances, you never want to get too close to wildlife. The animal can perceive you as a threat. In addition, you never want to touch them. Maintaining your distance is particularly important when they have babies with them. In these situations, they will be even more aggressive when you're in their vicinity.

If you identify animals as aggressive, maintain at least 100 yards between you and them. For all other wildlife, maintaining at least 25 yards is recommended.

Stay Calm and Never Turn Away from Wildlife

When you remain calm, it will help keep the animal at ease, making it less likely to attack. While you may be feeling anything but calm and relaxed, these are the feelings you need to display to the animal. This will reassure it that it's not being attacked or threatened.

In addition, there are very few exceptions to the rule that you should never turn your back on an animal in the wild. Many aggressive animals attack when their prey turns around, including mountain lions and bears. Some are also known for stalking their prey from behind, so it's a best practice to always be aware of your surroundings.

When confronted with a potential animal encounter, you must slowly back away without ever completely turning your back. At the same time, ensure you don't lose your footing and fall to the ground, making yourself vulnerable. After you get far enough away, the animal will no longer be interested in you.

Know the Animals You Could Be Dealing With

Before you head out on your wilderness adventure, it's best to be prepared by learning about the types of animals you could encounter. Learning about your potential enemy is essential for knowing how to handle the situation.

For example, if you're in an area with bears, you'll know you need to make extra noise while moving through the woods so that you don't accidentally startle one. On the other hand, if you're in mountain lion country, you'll understand the potential for being stalked by one of these big cats.

Keep Your Base Clean

Wherever you make your base camp, keep it clean. This means not leaving any food sources out where animals can smell them. Remove any waste from the area that could lure them to you. This will need to be done continuously after every meal. You don't want to have a surprise encounter while you're sleeping because you left the bones of your dinner next to your shelter.

RESPONDING TO AGGRESSIVE ANIMALS

There's no cut-and-dry response for responding to all aggressive animals in the wild, which is why it's so important to know what you could be dealing with before you head out on your adventure. How you respond to a potentially aggressive bear is completely different from how you will respond to an enraged moose. Learning the different techniques is essential to survival.

Handling an Aggressive Bear

You'll need to worry about two types of bears: black bears and grizzly bears. When confronted with a black bear, raise your arms and attempt to make yourself appear as large as possible. You'll need to create as much loud noise as you can. The goal is to try to scare the animal away from you. If these actions don't work and the bear attacks, don't play dead. Fight with everything you have inside you. Use your fists, feet, rocks, logs, and anything else you can reach.

When it comes to grizzly bears, the response is a bit different. Avoid eye contact and appear as small and unintimidating as possible. While remaining as calm as possible, attempt to back away unless the bear is approaching you. Do not flee if the bear charges or approaches. Instead, stand your ground.

If you have bear spray, be prepared to use it when the animal comes within 25 to 30 feet of you. Keep an eye on the bear's body language without making eye contact. An indication of a pending attack is having its ears back and head low. If a grizzly bear attacks you, it's essential that you play dead. Turn onto your stomach and protect your neck with your hands.

Handling an Aggressive Mountain Lion

If you meet up with a mountain lion, you must stop all movement. Don't try approaching the animal or fleeing. Try to enlarge your appearance as much as possible by spreading your arms. If you have a jacket on, spread that out too. If possible, stand on a large rock or tree stump to make yourself appear even larger. You don't want to do anything that will make you appear smaller, such as folding over on yourself, because this will make you appear more like prey.

Maintain eye contact with the animal and observe its behavior. If it maintains its location or approaches you, you should throw objects toward it but not directly at it. This should make it reconsider approaching any closer.

If the mountain lion attacks, trying to maintain your footing is critical. Unlike with a grizzly bear, you'll need to fight back. Use anything you have available. When they attack, they generally bite the neck and head, so protect both areas while facing the animal.

Handling Aggressive Wolves or Coyotes

Wolves and coyotes are pack animals, so it's essential to never get surrounded by the hunting party. However, there are some situations in which you could face a single animal. You'll need to treat this like facing off with a mountain lion.

Start by making yourself look as large as possible. While maintaining eye contact, begin backing away slowly. If the animal doesn't leave, make as much noise as possible to convince it you are a threat. You'll need to fight back if it attacks.

Handling an Aggressive Moose

Moose are generally not as aggressive as mountain lions; however, given the right circumstances, they can be deadly. You'll often have the opportunity to spot them before they spot you due to their massive size. If this is the case, back away quietly before you're seen. When a moose sees you, it's important to speak quietly and calmly, allowing the moose to know where you are while backing away.

Pay attention to potential signs of aggression, including stomping, grunting, and raised hair on the back and neck. The moose may charge at you in a ruse attack. Regardless of whether it's real or not, put something between the animal and yourself. If possible, it's best to climb a tree as long as you can get high enough where the moose cannot reach you.

While you should never run from a wild animal in most situations, a moose is an exception. They don't chase very far, so the odds of outrunning one is better than other animals. If a moose knocks you down, you should not try to fight back. Instead, curl into a ball to protect your vital organs and wait for the attack to stop.

UNDERSTANDING ANIMAL BEHAVIOR

Another important thing to understand before heading out into the wilderness is animal behavior. The first thing to know is that a startled animal will generally act aggressively because it feels threatened. To protect itself, it will frequently choose to attack you. That's why making noise as you progress through the woods is frequently recommended.

Second, if an animal has her babies with her, she will be extremely aggressive in protecting them. This means you'll have to be especially careful if you've come across a mother with her babies.

Third, turning and running from an animal typically initiates its predator-prey response. It will immediately recognize you as prey, even if you are not generally something that would be on the menu. Because of this, it's almost always best to continuously face the threat while slowly backing away.

CHAPTER ELEVEN: WEATHER AND NATURAL DISASTERS

The weather can severely impact your current situation and turn your pleasant day into survival mode. If you're expecting a natural disaster, you'll need to prepare as best you can to survive the storm.

Knowing how to respond to severe weather will make the experience much easier to handle. In this chapter, we'll explore how to prepare for natural disasters and respond to severe weather conditions. We'll also look at how to survive and take shelter if you're unable to leave the area.

PREPARING FOR NATURAL DISASTERS

To survive a natural disaster, it's essential to prepare. Having your ducks in a row will make you more likely to survive. One of the first things you'll need to do once you know a natural disaster is headed your way is create an emergency preparedness kit.

This kit should include everything that will help you survive the natural disaster, including the following:

- Three days of food, water, and medication
- Flashlights and batteries
- First aid supplies
- Battery-powered weather radio
- Manual can opener
- Sanitation supplies
- Local maps
- Baby supplies
- Pet supplies
- Dry clothing and blankets

Once you create this kit, keep it close to the door where you can grab it on the way to the car.

Prepare for Disasters Common to Your Area

When preparing, it would be best to focus on natural disasters known for occurring in your location. For example, if you live in Illinois, preparing for a hurricane wouldn't make sense. Instead, learn about the events that have happened in the past to prepare for what could happen again.

In addition, you'll also want to consider events like fires and floods, which are possible anywhere. Evaluate the situations that will require you to shelter in place and those that will require you to bug out.

Create and Practice Your Disaster Response Plan

The four major factors you'll need to focus on are where to take shelter, your evacuation route, how you'll receive emergency alerts, and how your family will communicate. Keep the following potential actions in mind as you devise your plan:

- Signing up for local severe weather alerts
- Programming emergency numbers into your phone
- Designating a family meeting place
- Planning escape routes
- Taking care of your pets
- Ensuring everyone knows how to shut off the utilities if there's a leak or other emergency

Make a Plan in Case You're Separated

Establish two places to meet up with your family. You should have one meeting spot directly outside your home and then one more somewhere outside the neighborhood in case everyone is required to evacuate. You should also choose an emergency contact person who lives outside of the area. Depending on the situation, it may be easier to use long-distance phone lines due to local lines being tied up.

Prepare for an Evacuation

You should also prepare for an evacuation and run a drill twice a year. Take your emergency preparedness kit and travel your evacuation route. Plot additional routes on your map in case one way is blocked. If you have pets, bring them on the trip, plotting out pet-friendly locations along the way.

RESPONDING TO SEVERE WEATHER CONDITIONS

You'll need to be ready to act when severe weather moves in. Now that you have a plan in place to respond to natural disasters, you can apply that to severe weather situations. No matter if the severe weather you're expecting is a tornado or hurricane, you'll be ready for action.

The first thing you'll need to do is decide if staying in place is the right thing to do. For a tornado, you don't have much choice but to shelter in place. However, if you have a hurricane coming, you'll have a choice to stay where you are or move to safer ground, depending on its severity.

If you choose to stay in your home, you'll need a safe room. You can use a storm cellar if you have one for wind-related severe weather. Otherwise, you'll need to find the most reinforced room in your home that's low to the ground. You'll also want to be in the most centralized part of the home that's away from windows and doors. Note that choosing the basement is not recommended for a hurricane due to the potential for flooding.

Severe weather isn't limited to these warm-weather occurrences. You could also face a blizzard that has you stranded wherever you are for days. You'll need to ensure you have all your resources prepared before the storm hits, such as food that doesn't require cooking, in case the power goes out. You could be stuck for several days with no electricity, so you'll need to be prepared with supplies to keep you safe.

It's not unheard of to be caught by severe weather while camping or at an outdoor event. This will quickly turn your fun afternoon or weekend into a survival situation. Before you go to the event, if there's a chance for bad weather in your area, have a plan for how you will deal with it should something go wrong.

SURVIVING IN EXTREME WEATHER

Whether you're at home or stuck in the woods, you'll need to take specific measures to ensure your survival during extreme weather. Severe weather can include anything from thunderstorms to blizzards. While you're in the woods, the weather patterns can change unexpectedly, so it's important to know how to handle yourself should the need arise.

Thunderstorm

We all know the best way to avoid lightning is to stay inside, but when you're in a survival situation, that's generally impossible. The next-best plan is to ensure you're not on a mountaintop where you could get struck by lightning. You'll also want to avoid standing at the base of single or isolated trees because those are more attractive to lightning strikes than large clusters.

While it may be scary to think about, most damage from electrical currents doesn't come from an overhead strike. Instead, it comes from the ground beneath you as the current travels from the strike point through the ground. Your goal will be to minimize the damage the current can do to your body should you be hit. To do this, keep your limbs tightly together while in an upright position. This will make the current flow through your body as quickly as possible.

You can also use that old trick of counting between lightning and thunder. For every five seconds you can count between the two, the storm is approximately one mile from your location.

Tornado

If you think there's no hope if a tornado develops while you're stuck in the woods, you're about to be surprised. Despite not having a perfect shelter to keep you safe, you can devise a plan to protect yourself from the dangers of a tornado so that you can ride out the storm.

You'll first need to find somewhere low to the ground such as a ditch or ravine. Then, using whatever you have on hand, cover yourself, especially your head. If you have a backpack with you, use that to cover your head, keeping it safe from anything that might fall on you. The main dangers of a tornado are not the physical funnel but the debris that's thrown around by the wind.

Blizzard

When you're facing a blizzard in the wilderness, you can make a cave out of snow if you have no other choice. However, it's better to find a deep tree well. You can build a fire using the dead wood you find in the immediate area. Even if the wood has been snowed on, it will burn, unlike wood that has been rained on. You'll need to ensure your fire is large enough to keep you warm against the frigid temperatures.

Flash Flood

Anytime you're near a river or in a canyon, you face the potential for flash flooding when the weather turns bad. It's essential to make it to high ground as quickly as possible to avoid getting swept up by the currents. Always knowing where your escape routes are is critical to being prepared in a worst-case scenario. Never try to cross a rushing river as it's rising. The currents can easily sweep you off your feet and carry you away quickly with deadly consequences.

SHELTERING DURING NATURAL DISASTERS

If you have the unfortunate situation of being caught in a natural disaster while out in the woods or somewhere similar, you'll need to find or create a shelter as quickly as possible. In most situations, trying to outlast the storm with no protection is unsafe.

In the case of a thunderstorm, you'll need to be particular with the shelter you construct. It should not be at the base of a single isolated tree. As we mentioned, this tree will be more likely to draw lightning than a cluster of trees. In addition, your contact with the ground is what puts you at risk of having current run through your body, so minimize your contact as much as possible by standing or crouching.

In a blizzard, we mentioned you can carve out a snow cave to make a temporary shelter. You'll need to construct it in a bell shape so that it's stable enough not to collapse on you. Then you can build a large fire near the entrance to your cave. Alternatively, if you have a tarp, you can construct a roof, but bear in mind that it will likely collapse under the weight of the heavy snow. If possible, find somewhere you can tuck into that's already formed such as a cave, overhang, or tree well. In any of these cases, you can build your fire right at the entrance, generating enough heat to keep you warm through the night.

For a tornado, there's really no option for building a shelter as anything you construct will likely blow away in the strong winds. Instead, find a ditch to ride out the storm. While experiencing a thunderstorm, it's good practice to look for somewhere to go in the event of a tornado since these storms are what generally bring them about.

CHAPTER TWELVE: SURVIVAL KITS AND GEAR

Survival gear is essential, much like a first aid kit. Having the right items in your survival kit will enable you to respond to emergency situations safely, quickly, and efficiently until you are rescued. Because you never know when you'll need it, you should take your survival gear with you whenever you go on an outdoor adventure.

Being prepared is the name of the game when it comes to survival situations. While it's possible to make do with all-natural supplies, it's a lot easier when you have tools at your disposal.

In addition, ensure your survival gear and kit are appropriate for where you're headed. For example, if you're going to the mountains in the winter, you don't want a survival kit geared toward the woods in summer.

In this chapter, we'll explore how to choose the right equipment based on your destination's environment. We'll also explain how to create your personal survival kit. Finally, we'll cover maintaining and repairing your gear so that it's ready for any situation.

CHOOSING THE RIGHT EQUIPMENT

When you're planning your outdoor adventure, consider the environment at your intended destination. It's important to have the right gear for the right conditions.

In the summer, the goal is to bring as little as possible to minimize what you'll need to carry. In the winter, bring extra of everything to err on the side of caution. At a minimum, you should think about packing the following:

- Extra clothes
- Polyester clothing
- Snowshoes and poles
- Topo GPS
- Personal locator beacon
- Hiking boots

- Rain gear

You won't need the extra clothes in the summer, and you can carry a smaller backpack than in the winter due to not needing as many supplies.

If the area you will be in receives a lot of rain, you'll need to pack your rain gear. Staying wet in any season is not ideal and can lead to sickness. In this situation, you'll also want a few extra sets of clothing in case you get soaked.

Consider the terrain as well. If it's known for being exceptionally rocky and uneven, pack appropriate footwear to ensure you don't have any preventable accidents.

CREATING A SURVIVAL KIT

When you create your survival kit, keep your destination in mind. Consider the weather forecast for the area during the days you'll be there.

Start by selecting a waterproof bag to protect your important items. Choose an appropriate size, which will depend on how many things you must carry.

Next, choose your fire starter. You'll want the type you're most comfortable using. For example, if you don't know how to use flint and steel, it's best to stick with a lighter or matches. Ensure it's safely placed inside the waterproof bag so that it won't get damaged.

Identify the area you'll visit and purchase a map that clearly illustrates the surroundings. Take some time to review the map to ensure you know how to read it and use the scale and special markings. Pack the map and the compass in your waterproof bag with the fire starter to protect them from the elements.

If you're going into cold weather, you'll need to prepare your clothing. There should be no cotton clothing in your wardrobe since it's more likely to hold extra moisture.

MAINTAINING AND REPAIRING GEAR

It's essential to have your gear in the best working order at all times. It would be terrible to get to your destination only to find your tent has a massive hole in the side when you're facing severe weather. Fortunately, there are steps you can take to maintain and repair your gear.

Keep It Clean

The first thing you need to remember with all your gear is to keep it clean. This means regular washings after multiple uses. Not only will it help protect your gear, but it will also keep it looking fresh for longer. Keep these recommendations in mind while cleaning:

- Ensure your washing machine doesn't have any built-up detergent in the dispenser that could damage your gear.
- Remove as much dirt and debris as possible before beginning the washing process.
- Use a specialty wash that won't damage the specific layers of the material, such as waterproofing.
- Read the care tag for information on washing and drying to ensure you're following all directions
- Wash specialty items separately, which can include any down jackets.

Reapply Waterproofing

Despite being called "durable water repellent," the protective coating on your gear is subject to wear over time with washings and use. Because of this, you'll need a reliable product that allows you to reapply a waterproof coating. Doing this will keep your gear going strong for much longer than not doing anything at all.

Clean and Store Your Tent Appropriately

Each time you return from a camping adventure, take some time to care for your tent. It's essential to treat this piece of gear right if you want to stay dry on your next outing. Follow these steps to maintain your tent:

- At home, set your tent up in a dry location where any remaining moisture can air dry.
- Remove any dirt and debris you can see and spot clean as necessary.
- Inspect for small holes and other defects that you'll need to address now to have your tent ready for the next trip.
- Fold your tent loosely to store in a larger bag instead of the compression sack as this will let it breathe.

Clean and Store Your Sleeping Bag Appropriately

Sleeping bags don't require washing after every trip unless they're severely soiled. However, they will eventually need to be washed. Here's what you need to do to effectively and efficiently wash yours:

- Close the entire zip-up enclosure and fasten any Velcro tabs.
- Use a front-loading washing machine with a cleaner specified for down products.
- When drying, use the lowest setting until completely dry.
- If clumping occurs while drying, add a tennis ball to the machine to break up the clumps.

If it's not time for cleaning, you can unzip the sleeping bag and hang it outside to air out instead. Remove any dirt or debris and spot clean as necessary. Once it's completely aired out and dry, zip it up and loosely fold it into a larger bag. Don't use the stuff sack for storage.

Preserve Electronic Gear

You may not give much thought to your electronic gear when you're not using it in the great outdoors, but you've likely spent a lot of money on these devices. To help keep them going longer, you must remember to remove the batteries when storing them. Leaving batteries in the equipment can lead to leaks, which are dangerous and a nightmare to clean up.

Store Items in a Cool, Dry Area

Another thing to consider is where you store your equipment. The space needs to be cool and dry; otherwise, it's at risk for mold and mildew growth. Just when you think you're ready to head out on a new adventure, you'll find all your equipment needs to be thoroughly cleaned or, worse, replaced. If your home is in a humid area, you may consider adding a dehumidifier to the space, but you'll have to remember to empty it regularly.

How To Repair Holes in Waterproof Items

Even the most durable waterproof clothing has the possibility of tearing. The good news is you can repair it with waterproof tape. Follow these steps to repair your clothing for another day's adventure:

1. Ensure the area around the tear is clean and dry.
2. Lay the material on a flat surface.
3. Leave roughly 2.5 cm of tape around the perimeter of the tear and place tape over it to see how much you need.
4. Using scissors, cut the tape to the appropriate size.

5. Place the sticky side of the tape over the tear while pressing from the middle outward to ensure the fabric is smooth and all air bubbles are removed.
6. Allow it to set for 24 hours.
7. For the best results, apply it on both sides; however, internal application will prevent it from being seen.

How to Repair a Deflating Sleeping Mat

Does your sleeping mat deflate throughout the night? The most likely cause is a hole. The most difficult part of repairing a mat is often finding the hole in the first place. Follow these steps to locate the hole:

1. Mix water with a small amount of soap in a bowl.
2. Inflate your sleeping mat.
3. Sponge the soapy water onto the mat's surface.
4. Watch for the appearance of tiny bubbles indicating the location of the hole.
5. Remove the soap and mark the spot to be repaired.

If you can't find the hole using this method, you can also submerge the entire mat in soapy water. You'll need to squeeze it methodically to check for leaks. After you've found the hole, repair it with the following steps:

1. Ensure all soap is removed and deflate the mat.
2. Ensure the area around the hole is thoroughly cleaned and dried. (This step is crucial to the following steps, so be sure to do an excellent job.)
3. Apply a small amount of seam grip glue over the hole.
4. Create a 2-inch radius around the hole by spreading the glue.
5. Using the same waterproof tape you used for repairing your waterproof items, cut off the appropriate amount to cover the glued area.
6. Round the tape's corners and place it over the glue.

7. Use glue around the tape's perimeter to ensure it sticks completely.
8. Press firmly on the tape to ensure your patch sticks.
9. Let the patch set overnight, then inflate the mat to verify there aren't more leaks.

Pack a Repair Kit

When you're on your trip, it can be beneficial to have a repair kit with you. This way, if something happens to your equipment, you can fix it right on the spot. If you're able to do this, your gear will last much longer than waiting out the rest of your trip. Small tears in your tent or sleeping bag can easily grow into larger tears very quickly.

CHAPTER THIRTEEN: EMERGENCY PREPAREDNESS

Sometimes, preparing for an emergency means having a plan in place for your home. After all, not all survival situations happen in the wilderness. For example, if a Category 5 hurricane is coming your way, you can't just wait until it's on top of you to make a decision. Planning in advance for these situations will ensure that you and your loved ones are prepared for anything.

The first step is to make an emergency plan that considers all possible scenarios that could take place where you live. As part of that plan, you'll need to know how to properly stockpile supplies and understand when the time comes to evacuate.

One of the most essential aspects of emergency preparedness is understanding emergency procedures. They're in place to keep you safe and organized during a catastrophic event.

This chapter will explore all aspects of emergency preparedness to give you the best foundation for developing the ideal plan to protect yourself and your loved ones. We'll also provide an explanation of the proper techniques to stockpile supplies and how to tell when to evacuate. Finally, we'll cover the essential emergency procedures you need to know.

CREATING AN EMERGENCY PLAN

When preparing for a disaster, you'll need an emergency plan. In most cases, people haven't developed a plan or practiced how to implement it in the event that disaster strikes.

Consider the Needs Specific to Your Situation

The first thing you'll need to do is evaluate the area where you live. Consider what type of emergencies you could face, including natural disasters and other situations like house fires. You'll also have to think about the different family members living with you. Will you need to accommodate any special needs, such as those of senior citizens or small children? In addition, everyone's medical and dietary needs will need to be addressed.

Create an Emergency Supplies Kit

An emergency supplies kit is intended to provide you with everything you need for survival with no help for at least 72 hours. In the best-case scenario, everything will fit in one to two bags that are easily carried. Evaluate the contents of your kit annually to replace anything that has expired and update items according to the changing needs of your family.

Plan Your Safe Spaces

Each emergency will have different circumstances and requirements. Because of this, any safe space you choose will vary according to the specific situation. The first step to take is to identify all the safe spaces in your home. In the event that your home is no longer safe, you'll need a meeting place that's near your home where everyone can safely gather. If you need to evacuate, you must have a destination in mind and know the route you will take to get there.

Ensure Everyone Knows How to Stay Connected

Part of your plan should address communication. This needs to include how you plan to obtain local emergency alerts and how to remain in contact with your family members. Everyone must have emergency contact numbers stored in their cell phones, and it's a good idea to also carry a contact card with the same information written down. Include each family member's phone number, the police station, the hospital, and an emergency contact who lives out of the area.

If you're facing an emergency that's directly affecting your neighborhood, it's possible that reaching someone farther out will be easier, which is why you should designate a point of contact who lives out of town. All family members should know to remain in contact with this person to let them know they're safe.

Practice, Practice, Practice

It's not enough to have a plan. You need to practice it periodically as well. This will ensure that everyone is on the same page and knows the drill. You'll all be very comfortable with what to do should an emergency arise instead of panicking. Remaining as calm as possible in an emergency situation is the key to handling it well.

STOCKPILING SUPPLIES

When you have time to prepare for an emergency, it's important to stockpile supplies that will count. In addition to preparing your emergency kit, you'll need other crucial items such as food, water, a light source, and blankets.

As you plan out your supplies, remember that you'll need enough food and water for every member of your group to last at least 72 hours. For water, this comes out to approximately one gallon per person daily. You shouldn't save up things like soda, which can cause dehydration.

Consider the food items you store very carefully. They'll need to be shelf stable and last for extended periods. This will ensure they're available when you need them most. The following items are great ideas that can be used under most circumstances:

- Ready-to-eat canned goods, including meat, fruits, and vegetables
- Dry cereal
- Protein bars
- Peanut butter
- Crackers
- Shelf-stable milk
- Dried fruits

If your emergency involves a power outage, your refrigerator will only protect your food at the proper temperature for up to four hours, and that's only if you keep the door shut. The freezer will hold temperature a while longer due to everything being frozen solid; however, it can only maintain it for so long.

It's essential to monitor any refrigerated or frozen foods very carefully and discard them as they reach dangerous temperatures. If any food smells, looks, or feels off, it's better to err on the side of caution and discard it. There's no sense in adding food poisoning to the current crisis.

Additional items you'll want to stockpile include the following:

- Batteries
- Flashlights
- Blankets
- First aid supplies
- Over-the-counter medications
- Sanitary supplies (feminine supplies, diapers, wipes)

KNOWING WHEN TO EVACUATE

In case of emergency, it's essential to understand when it's necessary to evacuate. If authorities or emergency responders advise you to do so, it's critical that you act on their instructions immediately. Every emergency situation is different, and authorities will make their decision to evacuate on a case-by-case basis. They'll know whether it's safer for everyone to travel than it is to remain in place. In most cases, your indication that it's time to evacuate will come from an emergency broadcast or other notification from authorities.

However, if you detect smoke or hear an explosion or any other signs of danger, it's best to evacuate as soon as possible regardless of whether or not you've been given notice. Get as far away from the area of danger as possible to ensure your safety and well-being.

It's equally important to have a plan in place beforehand so that you'll know exactly what to do and where to go in case of an emergency. Always remember that your safety should be your top priority. That's why it's essential to write down the plan you develop and practice it with your family before an emergency actually happens.

UNDERSTANDING EMERGENCY PROCEDURES

Emergency procedures are essential for handling a serious situation. Authorities have developed these procedures to ensure the general safety of everyone involved and decrease panic and unrest. You can also develop your own emergency procedures to respond to specific situations.

Knowing what the procedures are is not the same as understanding them. Once you identify the procedures, it's essential to get a firm understanding of how they're intended to work. Some examples of emergency procedures and typical responses include the following:

- Medical emergency: Once you establish the unconscious person has open airways and is generally in stable condition, place them into a recovery position until paramedics can arrive.
- Fire: Safely evacuate with the least amount of smoke exposure and burns.
- Hurricane: Evacuate before the storm hits your area to avoid the greatest risk to life and safety.
- Tornado: Take shelter immediately in the safest place available to ride out the storm and protect yourself from debris and winds.

While there are many emergency procedures, you should familiarize yourself with the ones that apply to your location and any potential situations that could arise. You'll need to know what to do if a specific alert is announced, ensuring you respond appropriately.

CHAPTER FOURTEEN: LEAVE NO TRACE

When you head to the great outdoors, it's essential to make the least impact possible on the environment. We all play an essential role in protecting the natural world around us. While you may see litter on the streets as you make your way to and from school or other locations, that's not how it should be. Instead, when you're out in the wilderness, the goal is to leave it as you found it—pure and clean. It's not hard to spend time in nature and leave no trace as long as you are mindful.

In this chapter, we'll cover the importance of leaving no trace, including the seven supporting principles. We'll provide examples of how you can minimize your impact on the environment and cover how to dispose of waste properly. In addition, we'll discuss ethical considerations for outdoor enthusiasts.

THE IMPORTANCE OF LEAVING NO TRACE

To preserve the natural world, it's essential for humans to have the least impact possible on it. This prevents us from causing irrevocable harm. There are seven principles behind this philosophy that have grown over time from backcountry settings to envelop every kind of natural setting you can think of.

Plan Ahead and Be Prepared

It's crucial to have a plan for your trip. Start by learning the regulations for your destination. Depending on the season, you'll also want to prepare for extreme weather conditions, potential hazards, and any emergencies that can crop up.

Scheduling your trip around peak travel times and traveling with a smaller group can also help mitigate environmental impacts. Instead of bringing food in disposable wrappers, repackage it in containers that you'll take home to minimize the creation of waste.

Rely on a compass and map or GPS instead of other navigational tools such as marking paint or flagging.

Stick to Durable Surfaces

When you're navigating the terrain or finding the ideal place to camp, stick to durable surfaces such as maintained trails and designated campsites. A best practice is to build your camp at least 200 feet away from bodies of water. Remember that the ideal campsite is not one that you make—it's one that you find.

Dispose of Waste Properly

Littering is one of the biggest things to avoid when camping. It's essential that you dispose of your waste properly, including any trash you generate, solid human waste, and any soap used to wash yourself or belongings.

Leave What You Find

If you find cultural or historic artifacts, don't touch them. You can look at them and photograph them, but it's essential to preserve the past. You should also leave all natural objects as they were.

Reduce the Impacts of Your Campfire

When possible, avoid using campfires by relying on a lightweight stove for your cooking needs. Light can be obtained by using a candle lantern. In areas where fires are permitted, keep them small and only build them in designated fire rings. All wood and coals should be burned to ash and all fires put out completely. Once the fire is out, scatter the cooled ashes.

Treat Wildlife with Respect

Wildlife are not domesticated animals and should not be treated as such. This means you should only observe them from a distance. Additionally, you should never feed them. You can protect wildlife by keeping your food and trash stored securely. It's best to avoid wildlife during their sensitive times, including mating season and winter. It's also important to avoid introducing non-native species to the environment.

Be Respectful of Others

Be considerate of other visitors. They want to have a quality experience just as much as you do. Use respectful voice levels and avoid loud sounds.

MINIMIZING IMPACT TO THE ENVIRONMENT

Several things come to mind when considering how to minimize your impact on the environment. Following these suggestions will reduce the potential negative effects you could have while on your trip. Consider implementing as many of them as possible for the best results.

Make Your Own Snacks

Instead of purchasing individually portioned snacks and premade foods at the grocery store, consider packing larger portions from home in reusable containers. This way, you won't end up with wrappers and extra trash. In addition, you'll also save quite a bit of money by making your own food.

Don't Take Plastic Water Bottles

Plastic bottles are horrible for the environment. Many don't get or can't be recycled, and you can often find them lying around on the ground. Instead of taking these with you on your camping or hiking trip, consider a reusable water bottle. You can pack a water filtration device to ensure you always have clean water.

Avoid Water-Soluble Body Products

You'll probably have several different products for personal care, including bug spray and sunscreen. The problem with many of these products is that they're water soluble. Once the active chemicals get into the water, it causes pollution that can kill anything in the water that comes into contact with it.

Pack Out What You Bring In

Anything you carry into the natural world needs to be carried out. Because of this, it's highly recommended that you use reusable dishes that don't generate waste. If there aren't trash cans nearby, you're fully responsible for all your waste.

Camp in Designated Areas

Another excellent way to minimize your impact is by sticking to designated camping areas. When you start to branch out to areas not yet used, you affect the natural world. Designated spots are chosen based on several factors, including their durability and how safe they are for the world around them.

Follow All Fire Safety Guidelines

It's critical that you practice fire safety at every turn. While having a campfire is associated with the authentic camping experience, it's all too easy to have it go wrong one way or another. You should never leave a fire burning unattended or immediately walk away right after you extinguish it. All fires should be manageable in size so that you can control them.

DISPOSING OF WASTE PROPERLY

Waste is probably the biggest problem with camping if not handled appropriately. From your food wrappers to solid human waste, there are proper ways for disposing of everything.

As we mentioned, if you bring it in, you bring it out. You should plan on bringing trash bags so that you can securely collect any food wrappers. In addition, each camper will need a bag to collect their sanitary waste, including used toilet paper. While it might seem gross or disturbing, you can't leave it behind.

Solid human waste must be handled appropriately as well. In some areas, you may be required to pack out your waste. Even if not required, this is an option with available pack-out systems. If you're in an area that doesn't require packing out, dig a hole that's at least 200 feet from the nearest water source. This will prevent contamination of the water.

When you bring reusable dishes or bathe, you'll need to carry your water 200 feet from the water source. Then, using only biodegradable soap, proceed with washing. This is essential to avoid contaminating any nearby water sources.

ETHICAL CONSIDERATIONS FOR OUTDOOR ENTHUSIASTS

Outdoor ethics refers to the set of principles that guide our behavior in the great outdoors. These principles apply whether we're camping in a campground or backpacking in the backcountry. They ensure we minimize our environmental impact.

In addition, many of these principles allow us to have a safer, more enjoyable trip.

The primary ethical considerations for outdoor enthusiasts are the seven principles of leaving no trace. When you follow these principles, you'll have the least impact possible on the environment. From not disturbing the land to maintaining your fire at a reasonable level, you'll be well on your way to protecting the natural world around you.

Tread Lightly!® is a well-known national nonprofit organization emphasizing the need for responsible outdoor recreation. This organization offers principles that supplement the seven principles of leaving no trace. These principles include the following:

- Travel Responsibly: Remain on designated areas, roads, and trails. Don't attempt to go around obstacles since that will widen the trails. Instead, you'll need to go over them as best you can. Only cross streams when you come to a designated ford. Make every attempt to avoid wet and muddy trails.
- Respect Others' Rights: This includes owners of private property, other campers, and all trail users. You should leave any gates exactly as you found them. When someone is passing you or moving uphill, yield the right of way to them.
- Educate Yourself: Before your trip, you should collect travel maps and learn the regulations of applicable public agencies. In addition, consider recreational skills classes. You should also learn how to operate all your equipment efficiently and effectively.
- Avoid Sensitive Areas: These areas include wetlands, meadows, lakeshores, and streams. To do this, remain on designated routes. Doing this will help protect wildlife habitats and any sensitive soils from potential damage.
- Do Your Part: Always demonstrate the appropriate behavior when exploring the natural world. You should

- always leave the area you stay in better than how you found it, including minimizing fire use, properly disposing of waste, repairing degraded areas, and avoiding the spread of invasive species.

When you focus on ethical considerations while having a good time, you can have the best of both worlds. Enjoying your time in nature can be done without making a negative impact.

CONCLUSION

Whether you're camping, stranded, or experiencing an emergency situation, having survival skills is necessary to make it through with finesse. Being prepared for anything will allow you to remain calm, assess the circumstances, and come up with the best plan for the unfolding events.

Now that you have a basic understanding of outdoor survival skills, you can get a head start on preparing for whatever the future may hold. Even if you just want to prepare for your next outing at a campground, you'll be able to start your own fire and mend your equipment. In addition, with the right tools handy, you can even fish and prepare your own dinner if you're in an area that allows it.

Having first aid knowledge is also greatly beneficial no matter the circumstances. However, if you're stuck in a survival situation, it can be imperative to know how to dress a wound. Because we've covered the basics of first aid, you'll be more comfortable when faced with any of these situations. You'll also know what treatment options to avoid to prevent making the situation worse, including using a tourniquet incorrectly and causing improper blood flow.

In addition, you can help your family prepare an emergency plan in case of a disaster or other situation that requires a quick reaction. Understanding how to create a plan is essential to ensuring the safety of you and your loved ones. When you have your plan, you can help everyone run through it periodically to guarantee you're all on the same page.

One of the most critical things to maintain during a survival situation is your positive attitude. As research has shown, the most successful survivors are those who never gave up hope. Perseverance allowed them to remain strong, upbeat, and focused on getting out of the situation.

Now that you've completed this guide, you'll also be able to navigate through outdoor areas using several different methods.

Gone are the days of not knowing where you are or how to move forward. Getting some practical experience with a compass and map will ensure you know exactly how this method works while in the woods. While you're at home, explore the sky, looking for the markers we talked about. This will ensure you're familiar with what they look like and how they're positioned. You'll be a navigational expert in no time.

No matter the circumstances of being in the wilderness, it's essential that you have the least impact possible on the environment. Leave No Trace offers seven principles to follow that will help you minimize all impacts on the natural world around you. What you pack in, you must pack out, so choosing wisely when you prepare for your trip is essential. In addition, having great respect for wildlife and others in the vicinity goes a long way toward ensuring an excellent experience.

With all the knowledge you've gained, you can begin your journey of preparedness for any situation. When trouble strikes, you can be the calm-faced leader who keeps everyone's spirits up. With your understanding of how to build a shelter, find water, and signal for help, you'll be out of your survival situation in no time.

The best way to use what you've learned is to get hands-on practice. By actually doing some of the things we've covered, you'll gain practical experience and know-how that will allow you to become an expert. Dig out your old camping gear and inspect it for damage, repairing what you find. On your next family camping trip, start the fire using some of the techniques we covered. The options are nearly endless for what you can do.

Don't be afraid to explore the natural world to learn even more. Take this opportunity to stretch your adventurous muscles and gain more experience. What will be your next step?

Made in the USA
Columbia, SC
19 December 2024